MATHS PLUS

MATHS INVESTIGATIONS

Fully differentiated for the whole class

3

Series Editor   Len Frobisher

Writing Team   Jo Chambers
                 Len Frobisher
                 Jon Kurta
                 Jeanette Mumford

Heinemann Educational Publishers
Halley Court, Jordan Hill, Oxford, OX2 8EJ
a division of Harcourt Education Ltd

www.myprimary.co.uk
Help and support, plus the widest range of educational solutions

Heinemann is a registered trademark of Harcourt Education Ltd

First published 2003

08 07 06 05 04 03
10, 9, 8, 7, 6, 5, 4, 3, 2, 1

ISBN 0 435 02306 3

Illustrated by Andy Hammond
Cover design by Tom Cole

Design and layout by Artistix, Thame, Oxon

Printed in the UK by Ashford Colour Press, Gosport, Hants

Contents

Introduction

Maths Investigations

The National Curriculum of England (as those of Wales and Northern Ireland), together with *Mathematics 5–14* in Scotland, places strong emphasis on the importance of using and applying mathematics. *Maths Investigations* provides differentiated activities to engage the whole class and to develop the skills of all children in this significant area of mathematics. For each of Years 3–6 (Primary 4–7), thirty motivating investigations are set in a variety of contexts – real life, imaginary and mathematical. Each one allows children to become involved in the processes used to solve problems by:

- **communicating**, by means of appropriate mathematical language, tables and charts, and simple algebraic symbols

- **reasoning**, using a variety of strategies and leading, where appropriate, to making a general statement

- **decision-making**, undertaken in an informed and considered way.

Structure

The investigations have been carefully designed for use with the whole class. Each is structured in three parts, **Making a start, Main activity** and **Coming together,** supporting the three-part lesson of the NNS. An extension is also suggested under the heading **Taking it further**.

Making a start: a short, teacher-led introduction, to set the scene and discuss the initial part of the investigation as a whole class. In most instances a suitable context for the investigation has been suggested.

Main activity: children work individually, or in pairs or groups. This part of the investigation is structured to provide three levels of differentiation: *Core, Development* and *Challenge*. Each covers an aspect of the same investigation, but with increasing depth and demand.

Core: develops from the introduction in **Making a start** and is appropriate for all children.

Development: builds on work done in the Core and is suitable for most children.

Challenge: extends content, aiming to test the mathematical understanding and skills of more able children.

Coming together: bringing together any different ideas, patterns and solutions that have emerged. Children should be invited to describe and explain what they have done and, where appropriate, to suggest or explore general statements.

Taking it further: a line of enquiry based on the investigation, similar in concept to the idea of 'What if …?'

Teachers may find that some investigations take longer than others to complete. By its very nature, an investigative activity may develop in unexpected ways with different groups of children. The support provided should enable teachers to be flexible and to adapt the investigations to suit their class.

Choosing an investigation

In each investigation, specific aspects of mathematical content and problem-solving processes are targeted. The chart on pages 8–9 can be used to select an investigation that fits in with the programme of study for the class, either by matching the mathematical knowledge and skills of the children to the content as described in the second column, or by choosing a process or processes from the top of the table.

Charts on pages 10–12 link the investigations to the *NNS Framework*, *Mathematics 5–14* (Scotland) and *Lines of Development* (Northern Ireland).

A photocopiable Child Record sheet is provided on page 13. Teachers' comments could be used as a basis for planning children's future learning.

Description

For each investigation the left-hand page provides an overview, shows the problem-solving processes involved and outlines how to manage the differentiation. Tables at the top of the page highlight the processes targeted, and icons are used to indicate where in the investigation these processes occur.

This page provides an overview

Teamwork

Explore ways of allocating equipment during a PE lesson.

Resources
- none

Key vocabulary
describe, decide, share, organise, explain

Content
Using division and reasoning to allocate equipment.

Communication	Reasoning	Decision-making
• Discussing lesson planning • Describing/explaining decisions made • Drawing a diagram to show decisions made	• Considering ways of allocating equipment so that all children are occupied	• Choosing calculation methods and ways of organising the lesson

Making a start

- Describe how Mrs Baker is planning a games lesson for her class. She has 20 children and 5 footballs. Ask how she could share out the equipment and what she might ask the children to do. Encourage the children to describe activities as well as team numbers and allocations of equipment.
- Explain that Mr Clarke has 30 children in his class and takes out 6 footballs, 10 cones, 3 rounders bats and a tennis ball.

Main activity

Core	Children work in pairs to plan Mr Clarke's games lesson, detailing how he should share out the equipment amongst the children.
Development	Planning three different activities that each involve 10 children, so groups can swap activities without changing the group sizes.
Challenge	Organising a lesson in which Mr Clarke's and Mrs Baker's classes are put together and all the equipment is shared out.

Coming together

- Invite children to describe their planning and organisation, and to answer queries from other children.

Process objectives for the investigation are listed

The investigation is structured in three parts

Three levels of differentiation are provided

Icons show where the relevant processes occur

48

The right-hand page provides in-depth support, including advice on the mathematical background and answers, where appropriate. It also offers suggestions for:

- what to observe while children are working

- ways to support children who may be experiencing difficulties

- helpful methods of recording

- discussion points and thought-provoking questions to ask.

Resources

Most investigations use readily available classroom materials. Copymasters to support teaching or recording are provided at the back of this book. However, many children will be capable of devising their own methods of recording, and should be encouraged to do so.

This page provides in-depth support and answers

Observing and supporting

Making a start

- Many children will suggest five groups of 4, each group having one football and perhaps kicking the ball to each other or playing a 2-a-side game. Children are used to sharing out equipment and carrying out similar tasks. Encourage different groupings and varied activities, for example, 12 children could play 6-a-side football while 8 children practise passing in pairs. List different football-type activities they could be doing to get children used to this way of thinking.

Main activity

Core   Ask children to consider games, skills, teams and equipment, and to draw a diagram showing the use of space, equipment and people. Children will come up with many different suggestions here. One example might be: 14 children (7 on each team) play rounders, using the 3 rounders bats, the tennis ball and 4 cones; one child keeps score and is the umpire. The remaining 15 children are split into 3 groups of 5 children; each group has 2 footballs and 2 cones. They set up the cones as a goal and practise goal scoring.

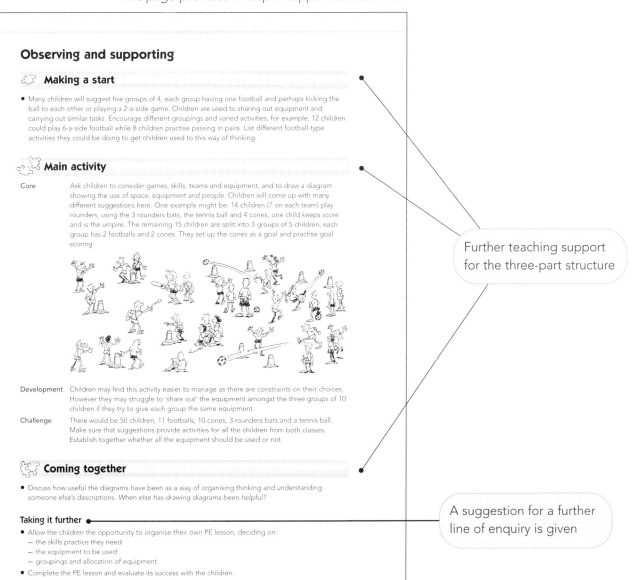

Development   Children may find this activity easier to manage as there are constraints on their choices. However they may struggle to 'share out' the equipment amongst the three groups of 10 children if they try to give each group the same equipment.

Challenge   There would be 50 children, 11 footballs, 10 cones, 3 rounders bats and a tennis ball. Make sure that suggestions provide activities for all the children from both classes. Establish together whether all the equipment should be used or not.

Coming together

- Discuss how useful the diagrams have been as a way of organising thinking and understanding someone else's descriptions. *When else has drawing diagrams been helpful?*

Taking it further

- Allow the children the opportunity to organise their own PE lesson, deciding on:
  - the skills practice they need
  - the equipment to be used
  - groupings and allocation of equipment.
- Complete the PE lesson and evaluate its success with the children.

Further teaching support for the three-part structure

A suggestion for a further line of enquiry is given

49

Problem-solving Processes Chart

Processes

	Communication									Reasoning												Decision-making				
	Modelling	Agreeing	Listing	Drawing	Recording	Comparing	Discussing	Describing	Explaining	Sorting/ordering/comparing/organising	Considering possibilities/explanations	Justifying/interpreting	Patterning	Using trial and error/improvement	Using information gathered/known facts	Predicting/estimating/testing	Finding all possibilities	Extending/applying /proving	Making/reversing a problem	generalisations/rules	Choosing units/equipment/scales	Choosing methods/strategies	Checking/testing	Deciding	Devising	Establishing
			•		•					•			•			•									•	
					•					•			•			•							•			
					•					•			•									•			
			•													•						•	•			
					•					•		•				•						•			
					•								•									•	•	•	
					•								•									•	•	•	
						•	•		•			•				•				•	•				
							•		•									•			•				
					•				•			•			•				•		•				
	•				•							•					•	•							•
	•							•				•									•				
								•					•		•						•				
	•											•			•									•	
								•					•	•			•				•				
			•				•		•			•						•			•				•
								•						•			•				•				
				•			•	•	•		•										•				
	•							•							•				•	•		•			
	•		•															•		•					
					•							•						•				•			
	•			•	•									•							•				
				•				•							•			•		•	•				
				•			•							•									•	•	
		•		•										•	•							•			
					•			•		•					•						•				
				•			•			•											•				
	•					•	•		•	•	•				•						•				
						•	•				•										•				
				•	•			•			•				•						•				

Maths Investigations 3 and the NNS Framework

Investigation	Page	Counting, properties of numbers and number sequences	Place value and ordering	Estimating and rounding	Fractions	Addition and subtraction	Multiplication and division	Using Money	Measures	Shape and space	Organising and using data
Long distance runners	14	●	●								
Charity envelopes	16	●				●					
Loading parcels	18			●							
Jumping frogs	20	●				●					
Face-to-face	22		●								
Where will I sleep?	24		●								
From post to post	26	●									
Can you halve it?	28				●				●		
Cube models	30	●			●						
Speedy deliveries	32	●				●		●			
Lucky dice	34					●					
Short Jack's silver	36	●				●		●			
Moving tiger cubs	38					●					
Take-away	40					●		●			
Bus riders	42	●				●					
On target	44	●				●	●				
Mind reader	46	●					●				
Teamwork	48						●				
Join-ups	50					●				●	
Filling the space	52					●				●	
Vegetable boxes	54				●					●	
Water carrier	56									●	
Slippery slugs	58									●	
Getting in shape	60									●	
Patterns with shapes	62									●	
Take your seat	64									●	
Program patterns	66									●	
Dolly Mixture	68										●
Bedtime	70										●
Bags of cubes	72										●

The solving problems strand is an integral part of all the investigations.

Mathematics 5–14 Guidelines (Scotland)

Investigation	Page	Information handling	Range and type of numbers	Money	Add and subtract	Multiply and divide	Round numbers	Fractions, percentages and ratio	Patterns and sequences	Functions and equations	Measure and estimate	Time	Perimeter, formulae, scales	Range of shapes	Position and movement	Symmetry	Angle
Long distance runners	14		●						●								
Charity envelopes	16				●				●								
Loading parcels	18					●											
Jumping frogs	20				●				●								
Face-to-face	22		●														
Where will I sleep?	24		●														
From post to post	26								●								
Can you halve it?	28							●			●						
Cube models	30							●	●								
Speedy deliveries	32			●	●				●								
Lucky dice	34				●												
Short Jack's silver	36			●	●												
Moving tiger cubs	38				●												
Take-away	40			●	●												
Bus riders	42				●				●								
On target	44				●	●			●								
Mind reader	46		●			●											
Teamwork	48					●											
Join-ups	50				●						●						
Filling the space	52										●						
Vegetable boxes	54				●						●						
Water carrier	56										●						
Slippery slugs	58										●	●					
Getting in shape	60													●		●	●
Patterns with shapes	62													●		●	
Take your seat	64														●		
Program patterns	66								●						●		●
Dolly Mixture	68	●															
Bedtime	70	●															
Bags of cubes	72	●															

As problem-solving and enquiry skills are an integral part of all the investigations, they have not been referenced here.

Lines of Development (Northern Ireland)

Investigation	Page	Length/weight/capacity/volume	Area	Time	Handling data	Number	Pattern/relationships	Shape	Space
Long distance runners	14					●	●		
Charity envelopes	16					●	●		
Loading parcels	18					●			
Jumping frogs	20						●		
Face-to-face	22					●			
Where will I sleep?	24					●			
From post to post	26						●		
Can you halve it?	28	●				●			
Cube models	30					●	●		
Speedy deliveries	32					●			
Lucky dice	34					●			
Short Jack's silver	36					●	●		
Moving tiger cubs	38	●				●			
Take-away	40					●			
Bus riders	42					●	●		
On target	44					●	●		
Mind reader	46					●	●		
Teamwork	48					●			
Join-ups	50	●				●			
Filling the space	52	●				●			
Vegetable boxes	54	●				●			
Water carrier	56	●							
Slippery slugs	58	●		●					
Getting in shape	60							●	
Patterns with shapes	62							●	
Take your seat	64								●
Program patterns	66								●
Dolly Mixture	68				●				
Bedtime	70				●				
Bags of cubes	72				●				

All the investigations provide suitable opportunities for children to experience elements of 'Processes in mathematics'.

Child Record

Name _____

Investigation	Comments
Long distance runners	
Charity envelopes	
Loading parcels	
Jumping frogs	
Face-to-face	
Where will I sleep?	
From post to post	
Can you halve it?	
Cube models	
Speedy deliveries	
Lucky dice	
Short Jack's silver	
Moving tiger cubs	
Take-away	
Bus riders	
On target	
Mind reader	
Teamwork	
Join-ups	
Filling the space	
Vegetable boxes	
Water carrier	
Slippery slugs	
Getting in shape	
Patterns with shapes	
Take your seat	
Program patterns	
Dolly Mixture	
Bedtime	
Bags of cubes	

Long distance runners

Funnel long distance runners into different tents by analysing the digits.

Resources

- enlarged Copymaster 1 (or OHT)
- number cards 10 to 99 (also for support)
- Copymaster 1 for each pair (plus some extra)
- Copymaster 2 (for the Challenge)
- 100-squares (optional)

Key vocabulary

predict, sort, units digit, tens digit, hundreds digit, even, odd

Content

Sorting and ordering 2- and 3-digit numbers.

Communication
- Recording 2-digit numbers in ordered lists

Reasoning
- Predicting how many numbers in each set
- Sorting 2-digit numbers according to whether the tens and units digits are odd or even
- Ordering 2-digit numbers
- Observing patterns

Decision-making
- Devising a strategy for sorting 3-digit numbers according to whether the hundreds, tens and units digits are odd or even

Making a start

- Display an enlarged Copymaster 1. Describe how children in a race are numbered 10 to 99 and funnels are used at the finishing line to sort the runners towards different 'finish' tents.
- Explain that child number 84 wins the race. Discuss which tent the winner will go into, taking an 84 number card along the 'units digit is even' funnel and then the 'tens digit is even' funnel to the correct tent.
- Repeat with the numbers 69, 12 and 37.
- Ask children to predict how many runners there will be in each tent when all the runners 10 to 99 are sorted. Record some of the predictions on the board.

Main activity

Core
Children work in pairs with Copymaster 1 to sort the runners from 10 to 99 into the appropriate tents.

Development
Putting the numbers in each tent in order. Another copy of Copymaster 1 may help.

Challenge
Investigating the number of tents needed for an adult race where the 3-digit numbers go from 100 to 999.

Coming together

- On your enlarged Copymaster 1, use children's answers to list the numbers in one of the tents in order. Discuss the patterns in the ordered numbers and why they occur.
- Challenge children to list the numbers in another tent in order without looking at their sheets.

Observing and supporting

Making a start

- When sorting 84, 69, 12 and 37, discuss the decision-making at each junction and which funnel the number goes into. Each decision requires understanding of place value, knowledge of which digit is the units and which the tens, and whether each digit is odd or even.

- Children will have previously met odd and even numbers in relation to the units digit. However, relating odd and even to the tens digit will be new. If necessary, cover up the units digit when discussing whether the tens digit is odd or even.

- Some children become confused when the tens digit is larger than the units digit. For example, they may say that 81 is even because 8 is even, and is larger than 1.

- When 84, 69, 12 and 37 have been sorted, talk about the odd/even nature of each digit in these numbers. Recording the information in a table like the one shown helps to explain why four tents are needed.

Number	Tens unit	Units digit
84	even	even
69	even	odd
12	odd	even
37	odd	odd

- Help children to predict how many runners in each tent by stressing that there are 90 numbers to sort and four tents in which they will go. Some children may make wild or nonsensical predictions. Remind them that a prediction is a 'good guess' that requires 'thinking'.

Main activity

Core   Some children may need to use number cards to aid sorting.

Look out for those who choose numbers randomly and fail to keep a record of which numbers they have sorted. (If necessary, suggest that they cross out each number on a number square as it is sorted.) Look also for those who work systematically using the funnels and those who put the numbers directly into the tents, ignoring the funnels.

A zero units digit can be a problem. Zero is an even number. Ask children to count back the even numbers from 10 to 0, or show them jumps of 2 on a number line to include 0.

Development   Encourage ordering of the numbers in their decades, grouping the tens, twenties, etc. This shows that there are five numbers from each decade in a tent, and observing patterns becomes much easier.

Challenge   Ask how many runners will be in each tent if all the 3-digit numbers are sorted into the same four tents as before. Suggest that more funnels are needed for the odd/even nature of the hundreds digit. Let children draw new funnels and tents before giving them Copymaster 2.

Coming together

- Emphasise how ordering the numbers helps show patterns in the odd/even tens/units digits of the numbers in each tent.

- Discuss why there are only 20 in two of the tents and 25 in the other two. (0 to 9 have not been used.) *Where would numbers 0 to 9 go?*

- Sorting and ordering of the numbers in the four tents results in:

11 13 15 17 19	10 12 14 16 18	21 23 25 27 29	20 22 24 26 28
31 33 35 37 39	30 32 34 36 38	41 43 45 47 49	40 42 44 46 48
51 53 55 57 59	50 52 54 56 58	61 63 65 67 69	60 62 64 66 68
71 73 75 77 79	70 72 74 76 78	81 83 85 87 89	80 82 84 86 88
91 93 95 97 99	90 92 94 96 98		

Taking it further

- Constructing funnels and tents for a race with numbers 1000 to 9999 (there are 16).

Charity envelopes

Investigate delivery of envelopes to houses with numbers that are multiples of 2, 5 or 10.

Resources

- enlarged Copymaster 3 (or OHT)
- Copymaster 3, two copies for each child (for support)
- 100-square (for support)

Key vocabulary

multiple, units digit, pattern

Content

Finding numbers that are multiples of 2, 5 or 10.

Communication

- Recording who delivers to which houses

Reasoning

- Sorting multiples of 2, 5 or 10
- Observing patterns
- Predicting which houses get 0, 1, 2 or 3 envelopes

Decision-making

- Choosing a strategy to work out which houses get 0, 1, 2 or 3 envelopes

Making a start

- Describe how Adam, Bess and Chloe deliver charity envelopes to houses numbered 1 to 50. Display this information:
  — Adam delivers to house numbers that are multiples of 2;
  — Bess delivers to house numbers that are multiples of 5;
  — Chloe delivers to house numbers that are multiples of 10.
- Ask who delivers envelopes to the houses with numbers 24, 15 and 30. Discuss why some houses will get more than one envelope.

Main activity

Core
Children find who of Adam, Bess and Chloe delivers to each of the houses numbered 1 to 50.

Development
Predicting, then finding, which houses get 0, 1, 2 or 3 envelopes.

Challenge
Working out how much money each child gets if they are paid 5p for every envelope they deliver.

Coming together

- On an enlarged Copymaster 3, use children's answers to show who delivers where. Discuss how the numbers for each child form number sequences. Together, look for patterns in the units digits of each set of numbers.

Observing and supporting

 ## Making a start

- Check children's understanding of 'multiple' before moving forward.
- Discuss methods used to decide whether 24, 15 and 30 are multiples of 2, 5 or 10. Some children may look at the units digit, others will use counting on, while some may use times-tables. Establish that they are equivalent, but that the units-digit approach is the most efficient.
- Ensure children consider all possibilities and are not immediately satisfied by finding that a number is a multiple of one of 2, 5 or 10. This is important in order to identify numbers, such as 30, that are multiples of more than one number.

 ## Main activity

Core

Some children may find crossing off numbers on a 100-square helpful, as they may choose numbers at random rather than working through 1 to 50 in order.

Encourage a systematic approach to the problem and a suitable method of recording. Focusing on Adam, Bess and Chloe (or multiples of 2, multiples of 5 and multiples of 10) leads to recording similar to this:

Adam (2): 2, 4, 6 …   Bess (5): 5, 10, 15 …   Chloe (10): 10, 20, 30 …

Focusing on each number from 1 to 50 in turn can be recorded in a table.

Copymaster 3 has been provided for any children not yet able to design tables. Each child needs two copies.

House number	Adam (multiples of 2)	Bess (multiples of 5)	Chloe (multiples of 10)
1	no	no	no
2	yes	no	no
3	no	no	no

Development

Ask children to predict how many of the 50 houses get 0, 1, 2 or 3 envelopes before they try to find out.

Systematic recording is helpful, though some children may need help to see how to go about it. Children who have used Copymaster 3 can head the extra column 'Number of envelopes' and count across for each house number.

Challenge

Children need to focus on how many envelopes each child delivers, that is, on how many of the numbers 1 to 50 are multiples of 2, of 5 or of 10. This also involves working with multiples of 5p. Adam gets 25 × 5p = 125p, Bess gets 10 × 5p = 50p, and Chloe gets 5 × 5p = 25p.

 ## Coming together

- Stress how important it is to record in a systematic way. Point out how Copymaster 3 does this and how it contains all the information in one table.
- Ask what is special about houses that get 0 envelopes (odd but not multiples of 5), 1 envelope (even but not multiples of 10), 3 envelopes (multiples of 2, 5 and 10). No house receives 2 envelopes, as a number that is a multiple of 2 and 5 is also a multiple of 10. End by discussing whether the rules for delivering the envelopes were sensible and what might be a better way.

Taking it further
- Delivering envelopes to houses with numbers 51 to 100.

Loading parcels

Sort parcels into vans by rounding numbers.

Resources

- enlarged Copymaster 4 (or OHT)
- number cards 10 to 24 for the teacher
- Blu-tack
- number cards 10 to 99 for each group (optional)
- Copymaster 5, multiple copies for each group (optional)
- number grid 10 to 99 for each group (optional)

Key vocabulary

nearer to, sort, half-way between, to the nearest ..., multiple of

Content

Rounding 2-digit numbers to the nearest 10.

Communication
- Recording which parcels are in each van

Reasoning
- Sorting parcels
- Observing patterns

Decision-making
- Choosing a strategy to sort to the nearest 20

Making a start

- Display an enlarged Copymaster 4. Explain that each of the numbered parcels has to be loaded into one of the vans. Point out the labels on the vans, *Nearer to 10* and *Nearer to 20*.
- Explain that the number on the parcel determines which van it should go into, and point out that the parcel numbers are being sorted to the nearest 10.
- In random order hold up each number card, other than 10, 15 or 20, to represent a parcel and invite a child to put it into the correct van.
- Do the same for parcels 10 and 20, and finally parcel 15.

Main activity

Core	Children sort parcels numbered 10 to 99 into 10 vans labelled in multiples of 10 from *Nearer to 10* up to *Nearer to 100*.
Development	Recording the parcel numbers in each van and the total number of parcels in each van.
Challenge	Investigating how to sort numbers 10 to 99 to the nearest 20.

Coming together

- Draw up the sorting grid shown on the facing page. Use children's answers to complete the 'nearer to 30' column with the numbers in order. Discuss any patterns children can see.
- Choose another column and ask what the patterns might be in this column. Put in the numbers to check.

Observing and supporting

Making a start

- Make sure that every child understands the concept of *nearer to*. A number line helps children to visualise it. For example, 23 is nearer to 20 than to 30:

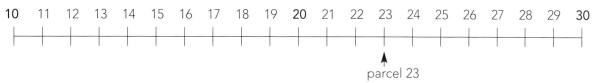

parcel 23

- Multiples of 10, such as 10 and 20, should be discussed as special cases.
- Odd multiples of 5, such as 15, create a difficulty. It is important that children are confronted with the dilemma of 15 being as near to 10 as it is to 20, i.e. half-way between the two multiples of 10. Children's views should be sought as to which van parcel 15 should be loaded into, thus highlighting the difficulty. Explain that such mathematical difficulties are resolved through the use of a rule that is reasonable and can be applied consistently without ambiguity. You could liken this to Mrs Watson, who is in charge of the delivery company, making the rule that 15 goes into the *Nearer to 20* van.

Main activity

Core As there are 90 parcels to sort, children could work in groups using number cards 10 to 99 to represent parcels. Decide whether an individual group can work out how they will do the sorting, or whether to offer advice. Copies of Copymaster 5 numbered 10, 20, 30, … 100 in the box may help some groups. Each group should decide who does what. Discuss this with the class before they start the activity.

Development There are a variety of ways that the sort can be recorded. You may wish to allow children to work in pairs to devise their own method. Two possibilities are:
- each number on a 10 to 99 number grid can be coloured to match a colour allocated to one of the 10 vans;
- every number can be recorded in turn in a table such as the one shown below.

Nearer to 10	Nearer to 20	Nearer to 30	Nearer to 40	Nearer to 50	Nearer to 60	Nearer to 70	Nearer to 80	Nearer to 90	Nearer to 100

Challenge You may need to explain what 'to the nearest 20' means. Challenge children to predict how many numbers are 'nearer to 20', 'nearer to 40', … 'nearer to 100'. They may be able to make the generalisation that the total number of numbers in each 'to the nearest *n*' set is *n*.

Coming together

- Draw attention to how many numbers are less than, equal to and more than 30, in the 'nearer to 30' column. Check that this is the case for every column.
- There are five numbers 'nearer to 10' and 'nearer to 100', but 10 in each of the other columns. Ask for explanations why this is. (Numbers 5 to 9 have not been used and they would go into the first column. Similarly, 100 to 104 would go into the last column, making 10 in every column.)

Taking it further
- Investigating rounding 3-digit numbers to the nearest 100.

Jumping frogs

Work out which stones frogs land on.

Resources

- enlarged Copymaster 6 (or OHT)
- toy or cut-out frog
- Copymaster 6 (for support)
- Copymaster 7, three copies for each child (optional)

Key vocabulary

jump, count on, predict, prediction, rule, multiple

Content

Counting on in 2s, 3s, 4s and 5s.

Communication

- Listing numbers in count-on sequences

Reasoning

- Predicting how many of the numbers 1 to 60 are 'count on 2' and 'count on 6' numbers

Decision-making

- Deciding how many stones each frog lands on
- Choosing a strategy to work out how many frogs land on each stone

Making a start

- Tell the story of four frogs, Twody, a 2-year-old, Threedy, a 3-year-old, Fourdy, a 4-year-old and Fivedy, a 5-year-old, who every day cross the river using the stepping stones (display an enlarged Copymaster 6). Each frog jumps according to their age. So Twody jumps in 2s, Threedy in 3s, Fourdy in 4s and Fivedy in 5s.
- Show the toy frog, Twody, on the left bank of the river. Ask children to predict how many stones Twody lands on while crossing the river. Record some predictions and discuss how sensible they are.
- Invite children to say which stones Twody lands on when jumping in 2s. List the number of each stone below the name Twody. Relate the numbers to counting on in 2s. *How many stones does Twody land on?* Compare this with the predictions.

Main activity

Core	Children list the stones that each frog lands on.
Development	Deciding how many stones each frog lands on, and predicting how many Sixdy, who jumps in 6s, would land on.
Challenge	Finding the stones that 0, 1, 2, 3 or 4 of Twody, Threedy, Fourdy and Fivedy land on.

Coming together

- Display a completed Copymaster 7. Discuss the 'count-on' number in each column and point out that it can be used to describe a rule. Recall that Twody jumps or counts on in 2s so Twody's rule is **count on in 2s** or **add 2**. Establish the rules for the other three frogs.

Observing and supporting

 ## Making a start

- Children may be confused between the size of a jump and the numbers on the stones. The first is a quantity, the second is a position. Look out for those who make a jump of 2 by missing out 2 stones, which is a jump of 3. This is 'stone counting' as opposed to 'jump counting'. All work using a number track, line or grid demands the understanding of this distinction.
- Some children may make outlandish predictions, for example that Twody will land on 100 stones. Ensure that they realise that this is impossible. Discussing predictions helps children to understand what a prediction is and develop the ability to predict sensibly and with a degree of accuracy.

 ## Main activity

Core
Some children may need a copy of the stepping stones on Copymaster 6 for support. Remind children to begin on the bank and not on stone number 1.

One method of recording is to list the stones that each frog lands on under its name. An alternative is to make a table of the stone numbers 1 to 60, as provided on Copymaster 7. Each child needs three copies, which they can complete using ticks/crosses or yes/no.

Stone	Twody (jumps in 2s)	Threedy (jumps in 3s)	Fourdy (jumps in 4s)	Fivedy (jumps in 5s)	Number of frogs
1					
2	✓				
3		✓			

The advantage of this table is that it retains the order of the stones 1 to 60 and all the information needed is readily available. However, some children may need considerable help in reading across rows and down columns to record and extract information.

Development
The total number of stones each frog lands on can be counted and recorded at the foot of each column. The product of the size of the jump and the number of 'landings' is 60 for each frog. This is true for any size of jump that is a factor of 60.

Sixdy, who jumps in 6s, would land on 10 stones.

Challenge
The number of frogs landing on each stone is recorded in the table but you may wish to ask children to list separately each stone that 0, 1, 2, 3 or 4 frogs land on. The number of frog landings is determined by how many of 2, 3, 4 and 5 the stone number is a multiple of. 60 is a multiple of 2, 3, 4 and 5, hence all four frogs land on stone 60.

Stones that 0 frogs land on: 1, 7, 11, 13, 17, 19, 23, 29, 31, 37, 41, 43, 47, 49, 53, 59
Stones that 1 frog lands on: 2, 3, 5, 9, 14, 21, 22, 25, 26, 27, 33, 34, 35, 38, 39, 46, 51, 55, 57, 58
Stones that 2 frogs land on: 4, 6, 8, 10, 15, 16, 18, 28, 32, 42, 44, 45, 50, 52, 54, 56
Stones that 3 frogs land on: 12, 20, 24, 30, 36, 40, 48
Stones that 4 frogs land on: 60

 ## Coming together

Take the opportunity to look for patterns in the units digits of each count-on sequence and ensure children relate these to being able to recognise multiples of 2 and of 5.

Taking it further

- Investigating other count-on sequences starting on the left bank and ending on stone 60.

Face-to-face

Investigate making 2-digit numbers from the numbers on two dice.

Resources

- two large dice with numbers (not dots) 1 to 6
- two 1 to 6 dice for each pair
- calculators for the Challenge

Key vocabulary

dice, face, opposite faces, predict, total

Content

Making and ordering sets of 2-digit numbers.

Communication

- Recording 2-digit numbers that are made

Reasoning

- Predicting the number of possible 2-digit numbers
- Finding all possible 2-digit numbers that can be made with like faces together
- Explaining why the total of each set of 2-digit numbers is 616
- Observing patterns

Decision-making

- Deciding how sensible predictions are

Making a start

- Hold up a large dice with the number 6 showing. Ask children to guess the number on your side, the opposite face. Invite a child to check and record *1 and 6 are on opposite faces*. Do the same for the 4-face and the 2-face. Establish what is special about each pair of numbers.

- Hold up the two dice with the 6-faces showing, then put the two 6s face-to-face. Record the digits that can be seen as a 2-digit number (the digits may have different orientations). Keeping the two 6-faces together, rotate one of the dice so a new digit appears, producing another 2-digit number. Do this four times until all possibilities have been found with the same tens digit. Discuss the numbers and what is special about them.

- Ask children to predict how many different 2-digit numbers can be made by rotating either dice with the 6-faces together. List the predictions and discuss how sensible they are.

Main activity

Core

Children make and record as many different 2-digit numbers as possible with the 6s face-to-face.

Development

Investigating the different sets of 2-digit numbers made from dice with the 1s face-to-face, then the 2s, 3s, 4s and 5s.

Challenge

Using a calculator to find the total of each of the sets of 16 2-digit numbers.

Coming together

- List each set of 16 2-digit numbers on the board. Discuss which digits are used in each set and which are missing. Ask for explanations why this is. Discuss any patterns observed within each set and between sets.

Observing and supporting

 ## Making a start

- On a normal dice the numbers 1 and 6, 2 and 5, 3 and 4 are on opposite faces, with each pair having a total of 7.
- When making 2-digit numbers you may need to refer to one of the dice as being in the 'tens' place and the other in the 'units' place to emphasise the place value of the two digits.
- When recording the 2-digit numbers made, write the numbers with the same tens digit beneath each other. This will suggest a systematic way of recording for children to follow.

 ## Main activity

Core

There are 16 possible 2-digit numbers with the 6-faces together.

Remind children of the importance of having a record of what they find out. Children frequently record in a random manner and they need examples and reminders in order to develop a more systematic approach.

22	32	42	52
23	33	43	53
24	34	44	54
25	35	45	55

Development

Tell children to write which numbers are face-to-face at the top of each list of 16 2-digit numbers. There are only three different sets.

The 6 or 1 faces together

22	32	42	52
23	33	43	53
24	34	44	54
25	35	45	55

The 5 or 2 faces together

11	31	41	61
13	33	43	63
14	34	44	64
16	36	46	66

The 4 or 3 faces together

11	21	51	61
12	22	52	62
15	25	55	65
16	26	56	66

This is because when the 6-faces are together the 1 digit is not available, since both 1s are on the outside faces of the dice. Similarly, when the 1s are together the 6s are on the outside. Thus the 6-faces together produce the same set of numbers as the 1-faces together. Similarly for the 5 and 2, and the 4 and 3. Let children discover this as they produce their own sets of numbers.

Challenge

Help any children who have not used a calculator before, stressing that they must be accurate in which keys they press.

The total of each set of 16 2-digit numbers is 616. Challenge children to explain why. The reason is that in each set of 16 numbers there are 8 pairs of units that each total 7, and 8 pairs of tens that each total 70, giving a final total of $8 \times (70 + 7) = 616$.

 ## Coming together

- When the 6s are together, both 6 and 1 will be missing, leaving the digits 2, 3, 4 and 5 to form all the numbers. As each of 2, 3, 4 or 5 can be a tens digit and each of 2, 3, 4 or 5 can be a units digit there are $4 \times 4 = 16$ possible 2-digit numbers.

Taking it further

- Investigating 3-digit numbers made from three dice with like faces together. There are $4 \times 4 \times 4$ (64) 3-digit numbers in each of three sets.

Where will I sleep?

Make sleeping arrangements for four children in beds placed in a line.

Resources

- enlarged Copymaster 8 (or OHT)
- squared paper for each child (optional)
- Copymaster 8 for each child (optional)
- number cards 1 to 4 (for support)

Key vocabulary

'next to' numbers, arranging, arrangements

Content

Sorting arrangements of the digits 1, 2, 3 and 4.

Communication

- Recording arrangements in order

Reasoning

- Predicting the total number of possible arrangements
- Finding all possible arrangements
- Finding 'next to' pairs in each arrangement

Decision-making

- Deciding how sensible predictions are
- Devising a systematic strategy

Making a start

- Describe how four children have a sleepover for Arthur's birthday but before they go to bed Arthur's dad sets them a problem. The four beds are side-by-side (draw up four rectangles to represent the beds). The four children are challenged to find as many different sleeping arrangements, one to each bed, as they can. To help them, Arthur's dad gives each child a different number, 1, 2, 3 and 4.

- Invite at least four children in turn to assign a number 1 to 4 to each bed. Discuss ways of recording the different arrangements. Ask for predictions of the total number of possible arrangements and discuss how sensible each is.

Main activity

Core — Children find as many different sleeping arrangements as possible.

Development — Sorting and ordering the number arrangements.

Challenge — Finding the number of pairs of 'next to' numbers in each arrangement.

Coming together

- Use an enlarged copy of Copymaster 8. Through questioning, build up the different arrangements for four beds in a systematic way.

Observing and supporting

 ## Making a start

- Children may record in their own way, discussing methods later. Squared paper is helpful, leaving space between each arrangement and putting arrangements below each other. Alternatively, Copymaster 8 provides a systematic recording structure.

 ## Main activity

Core

Some children may need a sketch of the four beds and number cards 1 to 4 to make their arrangements. Remind children to record each arrangement and to keep checking that each new one is different from any already made. Explain this is one purpose of recording.

Decide when to state that there are 24 different arrangements. Some children will want to know this at an early stage; others may become discouraged if they cannot find them all.

Development

Sorting and ordering highlights repeats and missing arrangements. Children will devise many ways of sorting and ordering. Discuss how useful each method is. One of the most useful is shown here. Cutting out each arrangement and sorting physically is helpful for many children. Recording on Copymaster 8 may make this more practical.

This method of ordering suggests a future strategy for similar problems. It also explains why there are 24 (4 lots of 6) arrangements. Whichever method children devise, ask them to look for patterns that help them explain the structure of the 24 arrangements.

First number ...			
... is 1	... is 2	... is 3	... is 4
1234	2134	3124	4123
1243	2143	3142	4132
1324	2314	3214	4213
1342	2341	3241	4231
1423	2413	3412	4312
1432	2431	3421	4321

Challenge

Explain that 'next to' numbers are those that are positioned beside each other on an ordered number line, or that have a difference of 1. Children may miscount how many 'next to' pairs are in each arrangement. Suggest that they work out a way of showing each 'next to' pair. One method is to link pairs as in this example, which has two pairs:

2̂3̂41

When children have found the number of 'next to' pairs in every arrangement they can sort them according to the number.

Ask children to look for patterns in the table. One particularly interesting one is to find reversals and where they are sorted. For example 2413 and 3142 are reversals, both with no 'next to' pairs. Let children explain what they discover.

Number of 'next to' pairs ...			
... is 0	... is 1	... is 2	... is 3
2413	1324	1243	1234
3142	1342	1432	4321
	1423	2134	
	2314	2143	
	2431	2341	
	3124	3214	
	3241	3412	
	4132	3421	
	4213	4123	
	4231	4312	

Coming together

- Ask children to describe any patterns they can see. Observing and describing patterns helps children understand the structure of the solution and suggests strategies for future use in similar problems.

Taking it further

- Finding different arrangements in which four children could sleep if the beds were placed in a circle or a cross.

From post to post

Move around the game board to make number sequences.

Resources

- enlarged 3-position board from Copymaster 9 (or OHT)
- 3-position board from Copymaster 9 for each child
- counter for each child
- Copymaster 10 for each child (plus some extra)
- 4-position board from Copymaster 9 for 'Taking it further'

Key vocabulary

start position, count on, repeating sequence, pattern, clockwise, anticlockwise

Content

Making and investigating repeating number sequences.

Communication
- Recording sequences made

Reasoning
- Observing pattern
- Using pattern to extend a repeating sequence

Decision-making
- Devising sequences using anticlockwise moves
- Deciding how to match and sort sequences

Making a start

- Display an enlarged 3-position board from Copymaster 9. Explain that this is a game board. A player decides where to start and chooses a count-on number, for example start on 2 and count on 2. Record the start number and use the count-on number to make clockwise moves, recording the number you get to after each count on. Ask a child to make the moves and establish the sequence of numbers produced (2 1 3 2 1 3 …). After three repeats of the pattern 2 1 3, stop and ask if the sequence can be extended without making the moves on the board.
- Repeat the activity for start position 3, counting on 4 clockwise, and for start position 1, counting on 1 clockwise.

Main activity

Core   Children produce repeating sequences using different start positions and different clockwise count-on moves on the 3-position board on Copymaster 9.

Development Investigating sequences produced when the count-on moves are made anticlockwise.

Challenge   Matching and sorting the clockwise and anticlockwise sequences.

Coming together

- Question children to elicit the nine possible sequences. For each sequence ask for the start number, the direction of movement and what its count-on amount could be. Remember there are an infinite number of solutions. Also ask what the count-on amount could be if the same sequence was produced by movement in the opposite direction.

Observing and supporting

Making a start

- Ensure that children understand the distinction between numbers that indicate positions on the board and numbers that are count-on moves. There are only the three positions 1, 2 and 3 whereas the count-on amount is unlimited.

- If necessary, use a clock to revise the meaning of clockwise and anticlockwise.

- Encourage children to suggest how they might record each sequence. Point out that the start number, the count-on amount and the direction should also be recorded. For example:

  Start on 2 and count on 2 clockwise: 2 1 3 2 1 3 2 1 3 …

- Children could record sequences using Copymaster 10. Stress how this recording method organises each sequence in the same way and that this is important when recording information.

Main activity

Core
Give each child a counter and the 3-position board from Copymaster 9. Look out for children who quickly dispense with the counter or even the board as they recognise what is happening. Copymaster 10 may be introduced here if you have not done so earlier. Multiple copies of Copymaster 10 may be required.

There are nine 'different' clockwise sequences. For convenience, they are lettered A to I here.

A: 1 2 3 1 2 3 Start on 1, count on 1, 4, 7…   F: 3 2 1 3 2 1 Start on 3, count on 2, 5, 8 …
B: 2 3 1 2 3 1 Start on 2, count on 1, 4, 7…   G: 1 1 1 1 1 1 Start on 1, count on 3, 6, 9…
C: 3 1 2 3 1 2 Start on 3, count on 1, 4, 7…   H: 2 2 2 2 2 2 Start on 2, count on 3, 6, 9…
D: 1 3 2 1 3 2 Start on 1, count on 2, 5, 8 …   I: 3 3 3 3 3 3 Start on 3, count on 3, 6, 9…
E: 2 1 3 2 1 3 Start on 2, count on 2, 5, 8 …

In general, the same sequence is made from a given start number whenever the count-on amount has the same remainder when divided by 3.

Development
Discuss whether moving anticlockwise will produce different sequences. Children are likely to expect new sequences to be produced. In fact the same nine are made as when moving clockwise.

Challenge
To assist in matching and sorting, children can cut out their sequences from Copymaster 10. This enables them to physically move sequences, making matching and sorting easier.

Coming together

- Discuss in what ways the sequences A, B and C are the same and in what ways they are different. Do the same for D, E and F. You may wish to allow children to decide whether such sets of sequences should be considered the same or different.

- Children may notice, for example, that 1 2 3 1 2 3 … is made by starting at 1 and counting on in 1s clockwise or by counting on in 2s anticlockwise. In general, the same sequence is made from a given start number when the sum of the count-on clockwise and anticlockwise numbers is a multiple of 3.

Taking it further

- Investigating sequences made using the 4-position board from Copymaster 9. There are 16 'different' sequences.

Can you halve it?

Split a range of objects into halves.

Resources

- piece of string approximately 20 cm long
- Copymaster 11 for each child
- selection from: tubes/packets of sweets, chocolate bars, linking cubes, string, strips of paper, Plasticine, water, apple, orange, banana, bunch of grapes …
- rulers, scissors, pan balances and measuring cylinders

Key vocabulary

equal parts, fraction, whole, half, quarter, sharing, trial and improvement

Content

Comparing simple fractions in practical contexts.

Communication
- Discussing and comparing methods of halving objects and considering accuracy
- Explaining methods

Reasoning
- Testing ideas for halving objects

Decision-making
- Choosing methods for halving objects
- Choosing equipment

Making a start

- Show a piece of string (around 20 cm). Ask how it can be halved exactly. Discuss and test the accuracy of each method. Children should complete the 'string' section on Copymaster 11.
- Repeat the activity with an apple and then with a packet of sweets.

Main activity

Core
Each pair chooses a selection of discrete objects – packets of sweets, bunches of grapes, sticks of linking cubes etc. to halve.

Copymaster 11 may be used to record methods of halving and statements about the accuracy achieved.

Development
Finding halves of a lump of Plasticine, a glass of water, a banana.

Challenge
Finding quarters of quantities and objects.

Coming together

- Ask children to explain how they halved objects. Discuss the advantages/disadvantages of each method in producing exact (equal) halves. Some children may physically show their method.

Observing and supporting

Making a start

- 'Half' here is meant to be as exact as possible. Half is a mathematical term that has exactness but in practical situations it is often impossible to achieve this. Two methods for halving the string are:
  - folding, lining up the ends and cutting;
  - measuring, halving the measurement, marking half-way along and cutting there.

  These two methods – direct comparison and accurate measurement – should both be demonstrated clearly. They are both fairly accurate. Compare this with cutting the apple in half and weighing, which is unlikely to produce two equal halves, and with halving the packet of sweets, which, because the sweets are discrete objects within the packet, can be done by counting and sharing.

Main activity

Core

When halving an item made up of discrete objects, encourage children to make the connection with dividing by 2; children may need to consider what to do when the number of objects is odd. In some cases the 'left over' object can be cut in half (e.g. a sweet) but this might be less practical or sensible with 15 linking cubes.

Development

The methods here are likely to involve trial and improvement; for the Plasticine, children could break the piece in half, use a pan balance, then adjust. Alternatively they might roll the Plasticine out into a long strip and use a ruler to find a point half-way along. For the glass of water they can use a measuring cylinder or a second glass, pouring from one to the other until the amounts in both are the same (direct comparison). A banana can be cut lengthways as well as the more obvious way, half-way along its length (which is in itself difficult to determine). To be totally accurate, weighing is needed.

Challenge

To find a quarter, children should realise that they need to find a half of a half.

Coming together

- Discussion should focus on children explaining their choice of methods and justifying them in terms of how accurately an object was halved.

Taking it further

- Finding thirds of objects.

Cube models

Make a model with linking cubes that has a given fraction of a specified colour.

Resources

- model made from 12 blue and 12 yellow linking cubes for the teacher
- at least 30 linking cubes in 4 colours for each child

Key vocabulary

part, fraction, half, third, quarter, fifth, multiple of

Content

Recognising and finding halves, quarters and fifths of quantities.

Communication

- Discussing how to find out whether a model is half one colour
- Explaining how models have fractions of one colour

Reasoning

- Extending a simple problem

Decision-making

- Choosing a method for ensuring a model has the required fraction of one colour

Making a start

- Display a model of 24 linked cubes, half blue, half yellow, with colours arranged randomly. Discuss the model, asking how many cubes of each colour there are and what fraction of the model is blue. A half is likely to be suggested, maybe other fractions too, such as a third or a quarter. Ask children how they could find out what fraction of the object is blue. Repeat the questions for the yellow cubes.
- Ask a child to use the same blue and yellow cubes to make a model that more obviously shows half of each colour.

Main activity

Core — Children make a model that has half of one colour and half of another.

Development — Making a model that has four different colours, each forming a quarter of the whole, using a minimum of 20 cubes.

Challenge — Making a model that is one-fifth red, using a minimum of 20 cubes.

Coming together

- Ask children to show their models and to explain how they are sure that the model has half of each colour. Discuss which models can be checked by sight and which have to broken up for checking. Similarly, review the models that have other fractions of particular colours.

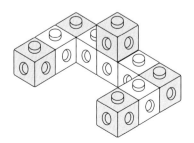
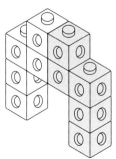

Observing and supporting

Making a start

- One important aspect of understanding fractions is to be able to recognise non-contiguous or 'disconnected' sections of a shape or object as being parts of the same fraction. In each of the three rectangles (right) half of the squares are shaded but not all are recognised so readily as such by all children.

- The initial model used should not be obviously half of each colour. The best way to show that the initial model is half blue is to count the total number of each colour. In order to do this it will be necessary to break up the model. Help children to establish that, since there are 12 of each, 12 out of the 24, or a half, are blue. Similarly, ask children to explain what fraction of the cubes are yellow.

- Models that are more obviously half of each colour are likely to have cubes placed contiguously, in a regular pattern or to have clear symmetry. If necessary, model this.

Main activity

Core

If children produce models with cubes of a particular colour placed contiguously, challenge them to rebuild models so that the cubes are non-contiguous – it is important to their understanding of 'a half' to recognise both situations.

Children should make a range of models requiring different numbers of cubes – encourage them to see that all their models have an even number of cubes, i.e. a number exactly divisible by 2.

Development

To make a model that is one-quarter of each of four colours, the total number of cubes must be a multiple of 4, i.e. 20, 24, 28, 32 … Any other number of cubes could not be split between the four colours equally.

Challenge

To make a model that is one-fifth red, the total number of cubes must be a multiple of 5, i.e. 20, 25, 30, 35 … Any other number of cubes could not be split into fifths.

Coming together

- Establish that a model that has half of its cubes any particular colour could have a range of different numbers of cubes in total, e.g. 20, 22, 24, 28, 32 … Ask what children notice about these numbers. *Would it be possible to make a half-blue model with twenty-three cubes? Why not?*

- Discuss how children can check that their models contain the required fractions of different colours and the fact that a model can be made to represent a half in many different ways.

- Children's completed models could be used for a classroom display; they should write a sentence for each, explaining the fractions of each colour.

Taking it further

- Making models with more complicated combinations of fractions – for example, a model that is a half red, one-third green and one-sixth yellow, or one that is a half yellow, two-fifths green and one-tenth blue.

Speedy deliveries

Send parcels using 2p and 4p stamps.

Resources

- enlarged Copymaster 12 (or OHT)
- cut out stamps from Copymaster 13 (for support)
- Copymaster 12 for each child/pair

Key vocabulary

combinations, same, different, total, predict, list, multiple of, order, fewest, repeat, addition, odd, even, divisible by, general

Content

Adding combinations of 2ps and 4ps to make different amounts.

Communication
- Recording findings in a table
- Explaining patterns noticed

Reasoning
- Looking for a pattern
- Making generalisations about parcels that can/cannot be sent
- Predicting which parcels can/cannot be sent

Decision-making
- Choosing a method for working systematically

Making a start

- Describe how the Post Office has only 2p and 4p stamps today but Jessica has three parcels to send. One needs 10p worth of stamps, one needs 11p and the third parcel needs 12p worth of stamps. Ask whether Jessica will be able to buy exactly the right stamps to send the three parcels today, or whether she will have to wait for new stamps.
- Ask children to work out which stamps Jessica needs to send each parcel.
- List systematically the different ways in which each amount can be made and establish which combination uses the fewest stamps. Record this combination on an enlarged Copymaster 12.

Main activity

Core   Children work in pairs to find the fewest 2p and 4p stamps needed to send parcels for amounts from 13p to 20p, recording their findings on Copymaster 12.

Development   Finding patterns in their table of results on Copymaster 12.

Challenge   Writing a general statement about the value of parcels that cannot be sent using 2p and 4p stamps.

Predicting which of the following parcels can be sent and which cannot: parcel A = 72p, parcel B = 53p, parcel C = £1·45, parcel D = £37·82.

Coming together

- Ask children to explain any patterns they have noticed in their results tables. Establish that odd-number amounts cannot be made.

Observing and supporting

 ## Making a start

- The 11p parcel cannot be sent, as 11 is not divisible by 2 or by 4.

Parcel 1: 10p	Parcel 2: 11p	Parcel 3: 12p
2p, 2p, 2p, 2p, 2p 2p, 2p, 2p, 4p 2p, 4p, 4p	cannot be sent	2p, 2p, 2p, 2p, 2p, 2p 2p, 2p, 2p, 2p, 4p 2p, 2p, 4p, 4p, 4p, 4p, 4p

- Help children to realise that the order in which the stamps are listed does not change the combination of values – for example, 2p, 4p, 4p is the same as 4p, 2p, 4p or 4p, 4p, 2p.

 ## Main activity

Core   Some children may need a set of cut-out stamps from Copymaster 13 to make the different combinations.

The ways of sending the parcels using the fewest 2p and 4p stamps are shown in the table below.

Development   Combinations of stamp values that are odd numbers, such as 15p, cannot be made because odd numbers are not divisible by 2 or by 4. Even numbers that are not multiples of 4 can be made using 2p stamps alone or with a combination of 2p and 4p stamps; multiples of 4, such as 16p, can be made in either of these ways or using only 4p stamps. For even numbers that are not multiples of 4, such as 18p, using as many 4p stamps as possible then adding a 2p stamp uses the fewest stamps.

Total	Stamps needed	Pattern created
13p	–	
14p	2p, 4p, 4p, 4p	1 × 2p and 3 × 4p
15p	–	
16p	4p, 4p, 4p, 4p	0 × 2p and 4 × 4p
17p	–	
18p	2p, 4p, 4p, 4p, 4p	1 × 2p and 4 × 4p
19p	–	
20p	4p, 4p, 4p, 4p, 4p	0 × 2p and 5 × 4p

Challenge   A general statement could be 'odd value parcels cannot be sent'. Some children may be ready to generalise further and state that 'odd numbers cannot be made by adding even numbers together'.

Parcel A = 72p and Parcel D = £37·82 can be sent as they have even-number values which can be made using 2p and 4p stamps. Parcel B = 53p and Parcel C = £1·45 cannot be sent using 2p and 4p stamps because they have odd-number values.

Coming together

- Invite children to explain why odd-number values cannot be made and focus discussion on two reasons. Firstly, odd-number values are not divisible by 2 or by 4, so they cannot be made by repeatedly adding 2 or 4 or any combination of 2s and 4s. Secondly, odd numbers cannot be made by repeatedly adding even numbers. Explore how this fact can be used to predict whether parcels with specific values can be sent today or not.

Taking it further

- Investigating which value parcels can be sent if there are 2p, 3p and 4p stamps available. Any value parcel can now be sent (except 1p).

Lucky dice

Investigate totals made when two or three dice are thrown.

Resources

- two 1 to 6 dice in different colours
- Copymaster 14 for each child
- enlarged Copymaster 14 (or OHT)

Key vocabulary

combinations, totals, same, different, add, most common, systematic, table, list, pattern, investigate

Content

Adding small numbers.

Communication

- Listing totals made
- Recording results systematically in a table

Reasoning

- Working out which total can be made in the greatest number of ways
- Extending the problem to three dice
- Looking for a pattern in the totals made

Decision-making

- Establishing that the same total can be made in different ways

Making a start

- Play the following dice game with the class. Ask each child to think of a number between 2 and 12 and write it down. Roll two dice and add the values shown to find the total. Anyone who wrote down this number gets a point. Record both the dice numbers thrown and the total made.
- Continue playing the game, recording the numbers thrown and the totals made.
- Draw attention to calculations that involve the same numbers in a different order, such as 3 + 5 and 5 + 3, and establish that here the same total is being made in two different ways.
- Ask whether children think all the possible combinations have been thrown or not.

Main activity

Core	Children work through the calculations in the two-dice chart on Copymaster 14 to show all the possible combinations.
Development	Using the chart to work out which total can be made in the greatest number of ways.
Challenge	Investigating totals that could be made if three dice were thrown.

Coming together

- Use the children's answers to complete an enlarged copy of the two-dice chart (Copymaster 14) and discuss any patterns they notice.
- *Which numbers would be good to choose as totals in the game?*

Observing and supporting

 Making a start

- Support with questions such as: *Which would be a good number to pick? Why do you think that?*
- After playing the game ask: *Are some numbers between 2 and 12 easier to make than others? How could we find out?* Take suggestions and lead the children towards investigating the different combinations that could be thrown and their totals. Establish that any combination of two dice numbers (1 to 6) is possible.

 Main activity

Core   Ensure that children understand how the two-dice chart on Copymaster 14 is set out. Explain how this shows a systematic approach and demonstrate how to read across the rows and up and down the columns in order to record all the possible dice combinations. For example, if the first dice is a 1, the second dice could be a 1 or a 2 or a 3 or a 4 or a 5 or a 6 – this is how the first row of the chart is completed.

	Second dice is a 1	Second dice is a 2	Second dice is a 3	Second dice is a 4	Second dice is a 5	Second dice is a 6
First dice is a 1	1 + 1 = 2	1 + 2 = 3	1 + 3 = 4	1 + 4 = 5	1 + 5 = 6	1 + 6 = 7
First dice is a 2	2 + 1 = 3	2 + 2 = 4	2 + 3 = 5	2 + 4 = 6	2 + 5 = 7	2 + 6 = 8
First dice is a 3	3 + 1 = 4	3 + 2 = 5	3 + 3 = 6	3 + 4 = 7	3 + 5 = 8	3 + 6 = 9
First dice is a 4	4 + 1 = 5	4 + 2 = 6	4 + 3 = 7	4 + 4 = 8	4 + 5 = 9	4 + 6 = 10
First dice is a 5	5 + 1 = 6	5 + 2 = 7	5 + 3 = 8	5 + 4 = 9	5 + 5 = 10	5 + 6 = 11
First dice is a 6	6 + 1 = 7	6 + 2 = 8	6 + 3 = 9	6 + 4 = 10	6 + 5 = 11	6 + 6 = 12

Development   Encourage children to look for patterns in the chart and to think about how they might usefully sort the information in order to show which total can be made in the greatest number of ways. The most common total is 7, which is made in 6 different ways.

Challenge   Starting from the completed two-dice chart and working out the totals if the third dice is a 1, a 2, a 3, etc. gives the possible totals shown here.

Third dice is a ...	Totals possible
1	3, 4, 5, 6, 7, 8, 9, 10, 11, 12, 13
2	4, 5, 6, 7, 8, 9, 10, 11, 12, 13, 14
3	5, 6, 7, 8, 9, 10, 11, 12, 13, 14, 15
4	6, 7, 8, 9, 10, 11, 12, 13, 14, 15, 16
5	7, 8, 9, 10, 11, 12, 13, 14, 15, 16, 17
6	8, 9, 10, 11, 12, 13, 14, 15, 16, 17, 18

Any total between 3 and 18 could be made with three dice. Ask children questions such as: *How many different ways can 10 be made with three dice? How can you use the two-dice chart as a starting point for this?*

 Coming together

- Establish that when several combinations give the same total, those totals are more likely to be made. Totals of 6, 7 or 8 are good ones to choose, because over many games they are likely to be thrown more often and so win more points.

Taking it further
- Finding out which total between 3 and 18 (made with three dice) can be made in the greatest number of ways.

Short Jack's silver

Investigate totals made with silver coins.

Resources

- boxes of 5p, 10p and 20p coins to represent three treasure chests or enlarged Copymaster 15 (or OHT)
- three 5p, three 10p and three 20p coins for each child (for support)

Key vocabulary

combinations, same, different, total, predict, list, describe, multiples of, order

Content

Making different amounts of money using 5p, 10p and 20p coins.

Communication	Reasoning	Decision-making
• Listing combinations available • Describing a pattern	• Predicting the additional combinations with an extra coin • Looking for a pattern	• Choosing a method for working systematically

Making a start

- Describe how Short Jack Silver and his band of pirates discover three treasure chests – one containing 5p coins, another containing 10p coins and the third containing 20p coins. State that the pirates can each choose two coins, either from the same chest or from different chests.
- Use children's responses to create a list of the possible choices and the total amount made by each. Establish whether choices that are reversals of each other are the same or different.
- Encourage children to be systematic.

Main activity

Core Children find all the total amounts possible if three coins are chosen.

Development Ordering the amounts made using two and three coins.

Challenge Predicting, then checking, how the list of total amounts changes if four coins are used.

Coming together

- Use children's responses to list and order the total amounts made with two and three coins. Ask children to describe the number patterns they can see. Ask why these patterns have been generated, and link them to addition of multiples of 5 and 10, and divisibility rules.

Observing and supporting

 ## Making a start

- You could use boxes of 5p, 10p and 20p coins for children to come and choose from, or an enlarged Copymaster 15 as a visual stimulus.
- When adding pairs of coins there are six possible combinations, shown here.
- Discuss whether 10p + 5p, 20p + 5p and 20p + 10p are new combinations or have been listed already as 5p + 10p, 5p + 20p and 10p + 20p.
- Discuss ways of working systematically (starting with a 5p and combining other coins with it, then a 10p and combining others with it whilst looking for repeats, and so on) to include all possible combinations.

Two-coin combinations
5p + 5p = 10p
5p + 10p = 15p
5p + 20p = 25p
10p + 10p = 20p
10p + 20p = 30p
20p + 20p = 40p

 ## Main activity

Core

Some children may need to use coins to help them find different combinations.

Encourage children to use the two-coin combinations to help work out three-coin combinations. For example, 5p + 5p = 10p so 5p + 5p + 5p = 15p; 5p + 5p + 10p = 20p; 5p + 5p + 20p = 30p.

Each two-coin combination produces three three-coin combinations. However, many are repeats, such as 5p + 10p + 20p and 10p + 20p + 5p.

Three-coin combinations	
5p + 5p + 5p = 15p	5p + 20p + 20p = 45p
5p + 5p + 10p = 20p	10p + 10p + 10p = 30p
5p + 5p + 20p = 30p	10p + 10p + 20p = 40p
5p + 10p + 10p = 25p	10p + 20p + 20p = 50p
5p + 10p + 20p = 35p	20p + 20p + 20p = 60p

Development

Ordering amounts made with two coins gives 10p, 15p, 20p, 25p, 30p, 40p. Ordering amounts made with three coins gives 15p, 20p, 25p, 30p, 35p, 40p, 45p, 50p, 60p.

Challenge

Remind children how the three-coin table can be used to help work out the four-coin table.

Four-coin combinations	
5p + 5p + 5p + 5p = 20p	10p + 10p + 10p + 10p = 40p
5p + 5p + 5p + 10p = 25p	10p + 10p + 10p + 20p = 50p
5p + 5p + 5p + 20p = 35p	10p + 10p + 20p + 20p = 60p
5p + 5p + 10p + 10p = 30p	10p + 20p + 20p + 20p = 70p
5p + 5p + 10p + 20p = 40p	20p + 20p + 20p + 20p = 80p
5p + 5p + 20p + 20p = 50p	
5p + 10p + 10p + 10p = 35p	
5p + 10p + 10p + 20p = 45p	
5p + 10p + 20p + 20p = 55p	
5p + 20p + 20p + 20p = 65p	

Coming together

- Discuss the coin combinations that can make the different two-coin and three-coin totals. Encourage comparisons of different combinations, asking: *Are these the same/different?*
- Ask children what they notice about the numbers, for example, they are all multiples of 5. Children may suggest 'it is the 5 times-table' or 'counting in 5s'. *How do you know these are all multiples of 5?* (They end in 0 or 5.) Extend by asking why the multiples of 10 also appear within these numbers. (Multiples of 10 are also multiples of 5.) Children may also notice that in the two-coin totals 35p is missing and in the three-coin totals 55p is missing. *Why? Which total would be missing if four coins were used?*

Taking it further

- Investigating which total amounts are made in two or more different ways.

37

Moving tiger cubs

Find different ways to move seven tiger cubs.

Resources

- enlarged Copymaster 16 (or OHT)

Key vocabulary

weight, heavy, heavier, combination, total, maximum

Content

Combining different weights.

Communication

- Explaining how the fewest trips can be made

Reasoning

- Testing out combinations of tiger cubs
- Using trial and improvement when working out combinations of tiger cubs for the trips

Decision-making

- Choosing methods for calculating weights and working out totals

Making a start

- Describe how Robin the Ranger needs to move some tiger cubs to a different Wildlife Park. He weighs the cubs before he loads the trailer. Display an enlarged Copymaster 16 and explain that there are seven tiger cubs weighing 26 kg, 24 kg, 23 kg, 28 kg, 29 kg, 22 kg and 27 kg to be moved. State that the trailer can carry only 85 kg and ask if all the cubs can be moved in one trip.

- *How could Robin move the tiger cubs?* Record and discuss some of the possibilities contributed by children, emphasising the number of trips involved.

Main activity

Core   Children find other ways in which Robin can move the cubs.

Development   Finding how Robin can move all the cubs in the fewest trips possible. *Is there more than one way to do this?*

Challenge   Robin decides to swap his trailer for another one so he can move the cubs in two trips. Children work out what weight the trailer must be able to carry.

Coming together

- Discuss the different strategies used by children to add cub weights.
- Compare different combinations to identify those that are the same and those that are different.
- Establish that the smallest possible number of trips is three but that there are several different ways to carry the seven cubs in three trips.

Observing and supporting

 ## Making a start

- The total weight of the seven cubs is 179 kg so they cannot all be moved in one trip. There are many ways to move the cubs but ensure that each trip totals less than 85 kg.
- You could point out that the total weight of the heaviest three cubs is 29 kg + 28 kg + 27 kg = 84 kg, which is less than 85 kg. This tells us that any three cubs can be moved in one trip. The total weight of the lightest four cubs is 22 kg + 23 kg + 24 kg + 26 kg = 95 kg. So it is impossible to move four cubs in one trip, but at any time any one, two or three cubs can be moved.

 ## Main activity

Core

This is an exploration stage during which children can discover that, dependent on the number of trips, certain combinations of cubs are impossible while others are totally open. To extend this, ask children to create lists of possible tiger cub combinations for a given number of trips. Here are some examples.

1 trip	Not possible						
2 trips	Not possible						
3 trips	Any three cubs			Any two cubs		Any two cubs	
4 trips	Any two cubs		Any two cubs		Any two cubs		Any one cub
5 trips	Any two cubs		Any two cubs		Any one cub	Any one cub	Any one cub
6 trips	Any two cubs		Any one cub	Any one cub	Any one cub	Any one cub	Any one cub
7 trips	Any one cub	Any one cub	Any one cub	Any one cub	Any one cub	Any one cub	Any one cub

Development
The fewest trips possible is three. There are many different ways to achieve this. Children might list a few of these ways.

Challenge
To move all cubs in two trips the truck would need to carry at least 95 kg.

Trip 1: 22 kg + 23 kg + 24 kg + 26 kg = 95 kg

Trip 2: 27 kg + 28 kg + 29 kg = 84 kg

 ## Coming together

- Explore small changes that create different combinations, for example, swapping two cubs round so they travel in different trips.

Taking it further

- Find all possible ways of transporting the cubs in three trips.

Take-away

Choose meals that cost as near to £10·00 as possible.

Resources

- enlarged Copymaster 17 (or OHT)
- Copymaster 18 for each pair (optional)
- selection of coins (for support)

Key vocabulary

list, choose, total, combinations, compare, addition, change, adjust

Content

Adding amounts of money to make totals up to £10·00.

Communication
- Listing elements that make up a meal

Reasoning
- Estimating costs of the total meal
- Using trial and improvement

Decision-making
- Choosing meals
- Establishing a good way of working out change

Making a start

- Display an enlarged Copymaster 17 and explain that it is a menu for Chinese take-away meals. Ask children to read the menu and think about the different parts that might make up a Chinese meal. List some children's chosen dishes for a meal, recording them under the headings starter, main course, rice, side order and dessert. Together, calculate the cost of the meals chosen.

- Compare different meal combinations and their costs.

Main activity

Core	Children work in pairs to select a meal each such that both meals together cost less than £10·00.
Development	Calculating the change from £10·00. Finding two meals that make a total closer to £10·00.
Challenge	Finding the smallest amount of money required to provide three people with a starter, main course and rice dish each.

Coming together

- Find out which pair's total meal cost was closest to £10·00. Establish that a good way of finding the change from £10·00 is by counting up in 1ps, 10ps and £1s (shopkeeper's addition).

Observing and supporting

 Making a start

- Allow additional time if children are unfamiliar with this type of take-away menu. Ensure children understand the elements that make up a meal, classifying the menu items into the five categories: starters (soups and appetisers), main course (chicken dishes, king prawn dishes and vegetarian dishes), rice, side orders and desserts.

- Establish that not all these categories will be represented in every meal, for example some people might choose to have a starter but not a dessert, or to have a side order instead of a starter. However, all meals should have a core element made up of a main course and rice dish.

 Main activity

Core
: Children could begin this activity using the meal choices totalled during 'Making a start'. Suggest they estimate the grand total as they make their choices. Copymaster 18 provides a format for recording choices and prices.

  Some children may need to use coins to support their addition.

Development
: Once the change from £10·00 has been calculated, children should adjust their meal choices, or parts of them, to make the total as near to £10·00 as possible. Some children may randomly select completely new meals each time to see whether the totals made are nearer to £10·00 (trial and error). They need to be encouraged to adjust existing choices instead, for example by exchanging one dish for a costlier or cheaper substitute. This process is trial and improvement.

  Some children may restrict their choices based on their real preferences. If this is the case, you may want to alter the context to avoid this: *Choose meals for two visitors that total as near to £10·00 as possible.*

Challenge
: The lowest cost would be achieved if all three people had the cheapest starter, cheapest main course and cheapest rice dish. This would be mushroom soup (£1·00), chicken and vegetables (£2·10) and (fried rice £1·10), totalling £12·60 for three people. Observe children who use trial and error, or even trial and improvement, rather than a logical approach and discuss this with them.

Coming together

- Find out whether anyone made selections that totalled exactly £10·00. You might explore how many dishes there are in children's meals and whether meals with more dishes are more expensive.

- Discuss the different methods used to calculate the total meal cost and how children knew by how much they needed to adjust the cost.

Taking it further

- Choosing two starters, two main courses and two desserts and finding out how many different meal combinations could be made from this selection. (Eight different combinations are possible.)

Bus riders

Find the number of bus passengers travelling each day.

Resources

- enlarged Copymaster 19 (or OHT)
- Copymaster 19 for each child
- number lines (for support)

Key vocabulary

total, sequence, steps, count back, decrease, fewer, adjust, trial and improvement

Content

Using addition, subtraction and number sequences to solve problems.

Communication

- Explaining in writing or with the aid of diagrams/ tables

Reasoning

- Using trial and improvement
- Extending the problem
- Looking for other decreasing patterns

Decision-making

- Choosing a method for calculating

Making a start

- Tell the story of Dave the bus driver who notices one summer that some of his regular passengers are walking instead of riding on his bus. He counts how many tickets he sells on his outward bus journey each weekday for one week. He counts 80 tickets in total for the week. Dave notices that each day fewer people use the bus than on the day before. Each day 4 fewer passengers use the bus than on the previous day.
- Display an enlarged Copymaster 19 and work with children using trial and improvement to find out how many people travelled by bus each day.

Main activity

Core   Children work out the number of passengers on Dave's bus each day if 80 tickets are sold for the week and there are 5 fewer passengers each day compared with the previous day.

Development   Finding out if it is possible to have a total of 80 tickets over 5 days with the number travelling each day being 6 less than on the previous day.

Challenge   Investigating whether Dave's 80 tickets over 5 days could be organised in other decreasing sequences of passenger numbers.

Explaining findings in written form or with diagrams/tables.

Coming together

- Consolidate children's understanding of number sequences.
- Explore patterns between the sequences with different step sizes.

Observing and supporting

 ## Making a start

- A sequence of five numbers that total 80 with a difference of 4 between neighbouring numbers is needed. The most suitable method for finding the sequence is trial and improvement, using existing knowledge of counting back in 4s to help.
- Having tried a sequence of five numbers, for example 20, 16, 12, 8, 4, total = 60, encourage children to make suitable adjustments. Here the total is too small so the sequence should start with a larger number. Try 28, 24, 20, 16, 12, total = 100, too large. The sequence needed is 24 on Monday, 20 on Tuesday, 16 on Wednesday, 12 on Thursday, and 8 on Friday.

 ## Main activity

Core

Children may find this more difficult if they are used to number sequences starting or ending with the 'step' size. With a step of 5, they may expect the sequence to start or end with 5 and be made up of multiples of 5. Some children may need to use a number line to support their counting back.

The sequence needed is 26 on Monday, 21 on Tuesday, 16 on Wednesday, 11 on Thursday, and 6 on Friday. Children should record their trial and improvement on Copymaster 19.

Development

The passenger numbers may decrease by 6 each day in the following sequence: 28 on Monday, 22 on Tuesday, 16 on Wednesday, 10 on Thursday, and 4 on Friday.

Challenge

The passenger numbers may decrease in steps of 1, 2, 3, 4, 5, 6, 7 or 8. Any step size larger than 8 gives a total larger than 80 for the 5 smallest numbers in the sequence.

Encourage children to work systematically through the different step sizes in order, and to record their findings in a clear and consistent way such as in a diagram or table.

Step size	Possible?	Passenger numbers
1	yes	18, 17, 16, 15, 14 (80)
2	yes	20, 18, 16, 14, 12 (80)
3	yes	22, 19, 16, 13, 10 (80)
4	yes	24, 20, 16, 12, 8 (80)
5	yes	26, 21, 16, 11, 6 (80)
6	yes	28, 22, 16, 10, 4 (80)
7	yes	30, 23, 16, 9, 2 (80)
8	yes	32, 24, 16, 8, 0 (80)
9	no	36, 27, 18, 9, 0 (**90**)

Coming together

- Clarify the main points drawn out from the activity: trial and improvement is a strategy that we can use to test out a sequence, adjusting it if the total is incorrect; sequences can start at any number and go forwards or backwards. Establish that these passenger number sequences decrease in steps of a constant size but that they can begin with any number.
- Use children's responses to list all the possible sequences in which Dave's passengers may have decreased over the week. Explore patterns within the results. For example, Monday's number increases by 2 on every increase of 1 in the step size; Tuesday's number increases by 1 each time; there are always 16 passengers on Wednesday.

Taking it further
- Investigating the sequences with a total of 80 tickets over 6 days.

On target

Find the scores in a beanbag game.

Resources

- two enlarged copies of Copymaster 20 (or OHTs)
- Copymaster 20 for each child
- multiplication charts (for support)

Key vocabulary

add, total, multiply, product, combination, score, odd, even, sequence, compare, patterns, systematic

Content

Selecting two of the numbers 2, 3, 5 or 10 and finding their product.

Communication
- Listing possible scores
- Listing systematically
- Describing a pattern

Reasoning
- Extending the problem using existing lists as a starting point
- Looking for a pattern

Decision-making
- Establishing rules for scoring

Making a start

- Display an enlarged Copymaster 20 and explain that Jason and Amanda are playing a game that involves throwing beanbags onto a target on the floor. In round 1 they throw two beanbags each and add the two numbers. *What possible scores could they get?* Together, create a list of all the possible scores.

- Discuss how to record a systematic list to ensure all possible combinations of numbers are included. The lower half of Copymaster 20 provides a framework for this.

- Discuss whether 2 + 3 is the same as 3 + 2 or is a different score, even though the total is the same. Establish what the score should be if two beanbags are thrown into the same numbered section.

- Display the list from round 1 throughout the activity.

Main activity

Core | Children find possible scores in round 2, when the two numbers on the target are multiplied. Establish how the results from round 1 can help in creating a list of the possible products.

Development | Comparing the two sets of scores (totals and products).

Challenge | Listing the possible scores if three beanbags are thrown and the numbers are added.

Coming together

- Invite children to explain how they found the scores in round 2. List these on your second enlarged Copymaster 20 and display them alongside the scores from round 1.

- Discuss the patterns, sequences and properties that children have noticed in the score lists from the two rounds.

Observing and supporting

 ## Making a start

- Discuss what 'systematic' means and show children how to use the table on Copymaster 20. Adding two numbers from 2, 3, 5 and 10 gives 10 different totals:

1st beanbag is a 2	1st beanbag is a 3	1st beanbag is a 5	1st beanbag is a 10
2 + 2 = 4	3 + 2 = 5	5 + 2 = 7	10 + 2 = 12
2 + 3 = 5	3 + 3 = 6	5 + 3 = 8	10 + 3 = 13
2 + 5 = 7	3 + 5 = 8	5 + 5 = 10	10 + 5 = 15
2 + 10 = 12	3 + 10 = 13	5 + 10 = 15	10 + 10 = 20

 ## Main activity

Core   Using the same combinations of numbers but multiplying instead of adding gives:

1st beanbag is a 2	1st beanbag is a 3	1st beanbag is a 5	1st beanbag is a 10
2 × 2 = 4	3 × 2 = 6	5 × 2 = 10	10 × 2 = 20
2 × 3 = 6	3 × 3 = 9	5 × 3 = 15	10 × 3 = 30
2 × 5 = 10	3 × 5 = 15	5 × 5 = 25	10 × 5 = 50
2 × 10 = 20	3 × 10 = 30	5 × 10 = 50	10 × 10 = 100

Children may record on Copymaster 20. Some may need to use multiplication charts.

Development   In the list of products the numbers are larger than in the list of additions, because multiplying two of these numbers creates a larger answer than adding them (or the same, in the case of 2 and 2).

In the 'additions' list there are equal numbers of odd and even scores, as 'even + even' and 'odd + odd' both give 'even', and 'odd + even' and 'even + odd' both give 'odd'. More of the products are even than odd, since only 'odd × odd' gives an odd product. Many products are multiples of 5, because multiples of 10 are also multiples of 5. Similarly, many of the products are multiples of 2, because multiples of 10 are also multiples of 2.

Challenge   Children should use the two-bag totals chart as a starting point, developing each combination into a set of three-bag combinations. The different totals are:

2 + 2 + n	2 + 3 + n	2 + 5 + n	3 + 3 + n	3 + 5 + n	5 + 5 + n	5 + 10 + n
2 + 2 + 2 = 6	2 + 3 + 3 = 8	2 + 5 + 5 = 12	3 + 3 + 3 = 9	3 + 5 + 5 = 13	5 + 5 + 5 = 15	5 + 10 + 10 = 25
2 + 2 + 3 = 7	2 + 3 + 5 = 10	2 + 5 + 10 = 17	3 + 3 + 5 = 11	3 + 5 + 10 = 18	5 + 5 + 10 = 20	**10 + 10 + n**
2 + 2 + 5 = 9	2 + 3 + 10 = 15	**2 + 10 + n**	3 + 3 + 10 = 16	**3 + 10 + n**		10 + 10 + 10 = 30
2 + 2 + 10 = 14		2 + 10 + 10 = 22		3 + 10 + 10 = 23		

Coming together

- Ask children to explain their calculation methods for multiplication.
- Encourage children to use correct mathematical language when describing any number patterns or properties. Discuss possible reasons for the patterns, sequences and properties that they see.
- Consider how the two-bag totals from the core activity could form a basis for listing three-bag totals in the Challenge.

Taking it further

- Investigating scores using two beanbags and different numbered sections e.g. 5, 7, 12, 13 and 20.

Mind reader

Work out the mystery number ... if you can!

Resources

- 100-square (for support)

Key vocabulary

total, product, odd, even, multiple, digits, properties

Content

Using division and multiplication skills.

Communication

- Explaining why a particular number has been chosen
- Describing a mystery number

Reasoning

- Looking for a pattern within a set of numbers
- Testing different numbers

Decision-making

- Choosing methods of working

Making a start

- Describe how Steve plays a game with his mum. Steve says, 'I'm thinking of a 2-digit number smaller than 50.' Ask children to suggest some of the numbers it could be. He then says, 'The digits of the number have a sum of 7.' Ask again: *What could the number be?*
- Record the numbers that fit Steve's criteria and ask children to explain their reasoning.
- Steve's mum says, 'I'm thinking of a 2-digit odd number. When the digits of the number are multiplied the product is 24.' *What could the number be?*

Main activity

Core	Children identify the mystery number that fits Steve's mum's criteria.
Development	Making up a similar puzzle then swapping puzzles and identifying a partner's mystery number.
Challenge	Making up a mystery number puzzle for which the possible solutions are 12, 33 and 54.

Coming together

- Discuss the solution to the core activity.
- Invite children who have completed the challenge activity to read out their puzzles. *Do they match the set of three numbers?*
- Establish how the core and challenge tasks require children to work in different ways to solve the problem.

Observing and supporting

 Making a start

- Possible solutions for Steve's puzzle are 16, 25, 34 and 43.

- Children may need to focus on each criterion in isolation, first thinking of a number less than 50 then checking whether the sum of the digits is 7 and repeating with other numbers as necessary. Some children may find a 100-square helpful.

- Establish that a useful strategy for finding Steve's number is to use number bonds to 7, starting with the smaller number as the tens digit and working systematically. Some children find it hard to keep two criteria in mind when answering questions and they may include 52 and 61 as possible solutions although they are larger than 50.

 Main activity

Core

Pairs of numbers that have a product of 24 are: 1 and 24, 2 and 12, 3 and 8, and 4 and 6. Only 3 and 8, and 4 and 6, produce 2-digit numbers when the digits are put together: 38, 83, 46 and 64. Of these possible 2-digit numbers, only 83 is odd, so 83 must be the mystery number.

A table can be helpful:

Pairs with a product of 24	Possible 2-digit numbers
1 and 24	none
2 and 12	none
3 and 8	38, 83
4 and 6	46, 64

Development

Children may find it easier to start with a number (the 'answer') and then consider its properties as a way of describing it. Encourage them to find just two criteria to define the number. For example, they could choose 45 and then fix the two properties as 'between 40 and 60' and 'with digits that total 9'. They should then try to solve the puzzle themselves, checking that their chosen number is the only possible answer. In this example there are two numbers that fit the given properties: 45 and 54. The child would need to adjust the criteria, in this case by making the two properties 'between 40 and 50' and 'with digits that total 9' to rule out 54.

Challenge

Properties that this set of numbers have in common include the following: 2 digits, smaller than 55, between 10 and 60, and multiples of 3. Children may be even more creative than this with their descriptions, but again encourage them to use just two criteria to set their puzzle.

 Coming together

- Discuss the strategies used. In the core activity children needed to start with 24, the product of the two digits that make up the mystery number, and list numbers that multiply to give this product. They then needed to consider the second criterion to select the correct numbers from the list.

- Point out that in the challenge activity they knew the set of solutions and had to think of properties shared by all three numbers. This involved working in the reverse order.

Taking it further

- Making up and solving mystery number puzzles with three properties in the description.

Teamwork

Explore ways of allocating equipment during a PE lesson.

Resources

- none

Key vocabulary

describe, decide, share, organise, explain

Content

Using division and reasoning to allocate equipment.

Communication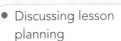

- Discussing lesson planning
- Describing/explaining decisions made
- Drawing a diagram to show decisions made

Reasoning

- Considering ways of allocating equipment so that all children are occupied

Decision-making

- Choosing calculation methods and ways of organising the lesson

Making a start

- Describe how Mrs Baker is planning a games lesson for her class. She has 20 children and 5 footballs. Ask how she could share out the equipment and what she might ask the children to do. Encourage the children to describe activities as well as team numbers and allocations of equipment.
- Explain that Mr Clarke has 30 children in his class and takes out 6 footballs, 10 cones, 3 rounders bats and a tennis ball.

Main activity

Core	Children work in pairs to plan Mr Clarke's games lesson, detailing how he should share out the equipment amongst the children.
Development	Planning three different activities that each involve 10 children, so groups can swap activities without changing the group sizes.
Challenge	Organising a lesson in which Mr Clarke's and Mrs Baker's classes are put together and all the equipment is shared out.

Coming together

- Invite children to describe their planning and organisation, and to answer queries from other children.

Observing and supporting

Making a start

- Many children will suggest five groups of 4, each group having one football and perhaps kicking the ball to each other or playing a 2-a-side game. Children are used to sharing out equipment and carrying out similar tasks. Encourage different groupings and varied activities, for example, 12 children could play 6-a-side football while 8 children practise passing in pairs. List different football-type activities they could be doing to get children used to this way of thinking.

Main activity

Core   Ask children to consider games, skills, teams and equipment, and to draw a diagram showing the use of space, equipment and people. Children will come up with many different suggestions here. One example might be: 14 children (7 on each team) play rounders, using the 3 rounders bats, the tennis ball and 4 cones; one child keeps score and is the umpire. The remaining 15 children are split into 3 groups of 5 children; each group has 2 footballs and 2 cones. They set up the cones as a goal and practise goal scoring.

Development   Children may find this activity easier to manage as there are constraints on their choices. However they may struggle to 'share out' the equipment amongst the three groups of 10 children if they try to give each group the same equipment.

Challenge   There would be 50 children, 11 footballs, 10 cones, 3 rounders bats and a tennis ball. Make sure that suggestions provide activities for all the children from both classes. Establish together whether all the equipment should be used or not

Coming together

- Discuss how useful the diagrams have been as a way of organising thinking and understanding someone else's descriptions. *When else has drawing diagrams been helpful?*

Taking it further

- Allow the children the opportunity to organise their own PE lesson, deciding on:
  - the skills practice they need
  - the equipment to be used
  - groupings and allocation of equipment.
- Complete the PE lesson and evaluate its success with the children.

Join-ups

Measure, join, fold and cut strips of paper and investigate results.

Resources

- coloured strips with lengths marked on them: 30 cm (red), 31 cm (blue) and 19 cm (white)
- enlarged Copymaster 21 (or OHT)
- Copymaster 21 for each pair
- Copymasters 22, 23 and 24 photocopied on red, blue and white card respectively, one set between each two pairs
- ruler, scissors and glue/sticky tape for each pair

Key vocabulary

metre, centimetre, half centimetre, distance between ..., distance to ... from ...

Content

Measuring to the nearest half centimetre.

Communication

- Modelling the problem
- Explaining results

Reasoning

- Testing predictions for different lengths of white strip
- Generalising about length of remaining part of strip

Decision-making

- Choosing lengths for red and blue strips

Making a start

- Invite children to measure and record the lengths of the three strips R (red), B (blue) and W (white). Establish that R is 1 cm shorter than B.
- Join the strips R to B to W to make one long strip. Calculate the length of the new strip.
- Fold the strip in half and cut it into two equal parts. Establish the length of each half.
- Show the half strip made up of R plus part of B. Ask: *How much shorter is the red strip than half of the total strip?* Cut off and measure the length of the blue part of this half strip.
- Complete the first row of both tables on an enlarged copy of Copymaster 21.

Main activity

Core	Each pair repeats the activity with strips R1, B1 and W1 from Copymasters 22 to 24 then completes the two tables on Copymaster 21.
Development	Repeating the activity with sets of strips 2 to 4.
Challenge	Predicting and testing what happens for any length of red strip (and a blue strip that is 1 cm greater) when the length of the white strip is 29 cm, 39 cm.

Coming together

- Ask children to describe what they found out. Ask: *Why is the length of strip that you have left over always 5 cm?*

Observing and supporting

Making a start

- Stress the accurate use of the ruler and check that children set the zero mark at the beginning of the strips.

- Emphasise the importance of accurate halving. Make a straight cut along the fold line.

- Cut off the red strip and measure the length of blue strip that you have left.

- Demonstrate each step in the problem, explaining which arithmetical operation(s) you are using and why, e.g.
  - I add 30 cm + 31 cm + 19 cm to find the total length of the strip (80 cm).
  - I divide 80 cm by 2 to find half of the total length (40 cm).
  - I subtract 30 cm from 40 cm to find the length that is left (10 cm).

| Red 30 cm | Blue 31 cm | White 19 cm |

Red ... Blue

| Red | Blue | → | Blue |

- Discuss methods of recording. Explain how to use the tables on Copymaster 21:

Measuring

Length of strips in cm		
Red	Blue	White
30 cm	31 cm	19 cm

Working out

Length of strips in cm		
Total of R + B + W	$\frac{1}{2}$ of total	$\frac{1}{2}$ of total minus R
80 cm	40 cm	10 cm

Main activity

Core — Establish that the tab at the end of each strip is to aid joining and should not be included in the measurements. Stress the need for accuracy when joining strips together and that the strips should always be joined R to B to W.

Development — Remind children to measure the strips to the nearest half centimetre.

Challenge — You may wish to ask children who have completed the challenge activity to find out what happens when the length of W is 49 cm, 59 cm, 69 cm … and B is 1 cm longer than R, e.g.

total is R + B + W = R + R + 1 + 49

→ $\frac{1}{2}$ of total is (2R + 50) ÷ 2 = R + 25

→ $\frac{1}{2}$ of total minus R = 25

Coming together

- You may need to direct children's reasoning by asking: *How might we use the fact that the blue strip is 1 cm longer than the red strip?*

- Stress the relationship between modelling the problem and the operations it illustrates, e.g. joining two then three strips (adding), folding in half (dividing by 2), cutting off the length of strip R (subtracting).

Taking it further

- Investigating what happens when you join strips of three consecutive lengths, divide the total length into thirds and compare a third with each length.

Filling the space

Find ways of filling the spaces in the decking of the boat.

Resources

- Cuisenaire rods of units 1, 3 and 9 for the teacher
- Copymaster 25 for each child
- sets of Cuisenaire rods of units 1, 3 and 9 (for support)
- Copymaster 26 for the Challenge

Key vocabulary

centimetre, distance between … to … from, measuring scale

Content

Using suitable units and measuring equipment to measure lengths.

Communication
- Modelling a problem
- Drawing diagrams

Reasoning
- Finding all possibilities by working systematically

Decision-making
- Choosing which lengths to use
- Establishing that some gaps are found by addition and some by subtraction

Making a start

- Establish the lengths of the Cuisenaire rods as 1 cm, 3 cm and 9 cm by asking children to measure them. Ask what other lengths could be made by using two rods together, and record some of the suggestions.
- Ask how the rods might be used to measure 2 cm, 6 cm, 8 cm.
- Introduce the problem by telling the story of Tom and his boat: *Tom needs an 11 cm length of wood to fill a gap in the decking of his sailing boat. He has lost his ruler. Earlier he cut three lengths of wood measuring 1 cm, 3 cm and 9 cm. How can Tom use his three lengths to measure 11 cm?*

Main activity

Core | Children find how Tom can use the three lengths of wood to fill a gap of 11 cm.

Development | Making drawings to record ways of using the three Cuisenaire rods to measure lengths from 5 cm up to 12 cm.

Challenge | A fourth length of wood measures 16 cm. Children find ways of using 1 cm, 3 cm, 9 cm and 16 cm lengths to fill gaps in the decking between 13 cm and 29 cm.

Coming together

- Establish how Tom filled the gap in his decking and invite children to draw up diagrams for some of the other gaps up to 12 cm.
- Discuss different solutions for gaps of 6 cm, 7 cm, 10 cm and 13 cm when a 16 cm rod is included in the set of rods.
- Model solutions to the Challenge activity that use four rods.

Observing and supporting

Making a start

- You may want to ask children to write the length on each rod.
- The idea of using Cuisenaire materials for addition and subtraction may be new to the class.
- Establish that rods laid end to end model the operation of addition and that the order of the rods is unimportant, e.g. 9 cm + 3 cm = 3 cm + 9 cm.

9 cm	3 cm
12 cm	

- When the solution is found by subtraction, some children may find it helpful to measure the 'difference'.

3 cm	9 cm	9 cm
1 cm ← 2 cm →	3 cm ← 6 cm →	1 cm ← 8 cm →

- After telling the story, ask children what information they have and what they need to find out.

Main activity

Core and Development

You may want to suggest that children record the lengths on Copymaster 25 by drawing round the Cuisenaire rods. The Copymaster promotes a systematic approach where the length of gap increases by 1 cm each time, leading to these results:

Length of gap	Number of lengths used	How used	Operation
5 cm	3	9 cm – 3 cm – 1 cm	–, –
6 cm	2	9 cm – 3 cm	–
7 cm	3	9 cm + 1 cm – 3 cm	+, –
8 cm	2	9 cm – 1 cm	–
9 cm	1	9 cm	
10 cm	2	9 cm + 1 cm	+
11 cm	3	9 cm + 3 cm – 1 cm	+, –
12 cm	2	9 cm + 3 cm	+

Challenge

Ask children to complete Copymaster 26. They may sketch the rods or note the measurements and operations used.

Coming together

- 6 cm can be made as 9 – 3 or 16 – 9 – 1; 7 cm can be made as (9 + 1) – 3 or 16 – 9; 10 cm can be made as 9 + 1 or (16 + 3) – 9; and 13 can be made as 9 + 3 + 1 or 16 – 3.
- Choose children to model and sketch four-rod solutions:

16 cm	9 cm	
1 cm	3 cm ← 21 cm →	

16 cm	9 cm	1 cm
3 cm ← 23 cm →		

16 cm	9 cm	3 cm
1 cm ← 27 cm →		

Taking it further

- Investigating which whole-centimetre lengths between 30 cm and 40 cm can be measured when two of each of the rods 1 cm, 4 cm, 9 cm and 16 cm are available.

Vegetable boxes

Find the weights of vegetable boxes containing different types of vegetable.

Resources

- cards labelled:
  potatoes 3 kg,
  onions $1\frac{1}{2}$ kg,
  carrots 1 kg,
  leeks $\frac{1}{2}$ kg,
  mushrooms $\frac{1}{4}$ kg
- scales marked in
  $\frac{1}{4}$ kg intervals
- enlarged
  Copymaster 27
  (or OHT)
- Copymaster 27
  for each child

Key vocabulary

kilogram, half
kilogram, quarter
kilogram, scales,
weight

Content

Reading scales to the nearest division and calculating total weights.

Communication
- Recording all the possible combinations of vegetables

Reasoning
- Looking for a pattern in the organised list
- Extending the problem to other types of vegetable boxes

Decision-making
- Checking results

Making a start

- Describe how Highland Organic Farm sells boxes containing bags of different vegetables. Display the five cards, explaining that they show the weights of a bag of each vegetable. Depress the scales to a marked division, such as 3 kg, and ask children to identify which vegetable has this bagged weight. (potatoes)
- Say that Lachie fills a box with a bag each of potatoes, onions, carrots and leeks. Ask what the contents of his 4-vegetable box will weigh on the scales. (3 kg + $1\frac{1}{2}$ kg + 1 kg + $\frac{1}{2}$ kg = 6 kg)
- Discuss methods of recording. Display an enlarged Copymaster 27 and model how to record Lachie's vegetable box, with ticks in the relevant boxes.
- Ask for suggestions for 4 out of the 5 vegetables to fill another box. Elicit three examples from the children.

Main activity

Core   Children work in pairs to find all the possible 4-vegetable boxes and the weight of the contents of each box.

Development   Finding the different boxes, and their weights, that can be made from 3 of the 5 types of vegetable.

Challenge   Finding the total number of 1-, 2-, 3-, 4- and 5-vegetable boxes that can be made from the 5 types of vegetable.

Coming together

- Establish and list all the possible 4-vegetable boxes, asking children to describe any patterns they notice.
- Establish and list the 10 possible 3-vegetable boxes and weights. Begin with potatoes and 2 others (6 ways), then no potatoes but onions and 2 others (3 ways), then no potatoes or onions (1 way).
- Discuss how making an organised list helps us check our results.
- Invite reports from children who completed the Challenge.

Observing and supporting

Making a start

- Check that children know that $\frac{1}{2}$ kg + $\frac{1}{2}$ kg = 1 kg and $\frac{1}{2}$ kg + $\frac{1}{4}$ kg = $\frac{3}{4}$ kg. Establish and compare mental methods for totalling weights, e.g. 3 kg + $\frac{1}{2}$ kg + 1$\frac{1}{2}$ kg + $\frac{1}{4}$ kg.
- Encourage children to think of **a** bag of … rather than **one** bag of … They should record each bag as a dot or tick, not a number. This will help them to see the pattern in the list and encourage the use of mental methods.

Bag of potatoes	Bag of onions	Bag of carrots	Bag of leeks	Bag of mushrooms	Total weight
•	•	•	•		6 kg

Main activity

Core   You may want to suggest that children begin their list with potatoes.

Potatoes	Onions	Carrots	Leeks	Mushrooms	Weight
•	•	•	•		6 kg
•	•	•		•	5$\frac{3}{4}$ kg
•	•		•	•	5$\frac{1}{4}$ kg
•		•	•	•	4$\frac{3}{4}$ kg
	•	•	•	•	3$\frac{1}{4}$ kg

Development   You may want to suggest that children find all the 3-vegetable boxes that have potatoes, then those that have no potatoes.

Potatoes	Onions	Carrots	Leeks	Mushrooms	Weight
•	•	•			5$\frac{1}{2}$ kg
•	•		•		5 kg
•	•			•	4$\frac{3}{4}$ kg
•		•	•		4$\frac{1}{2}$ kg
•		•		•	4$\frac{1}{4}$ kg
•			•	•	3$\frac{3}{4}$ kg
	•	•	•		3 kg
	•	•		•	2$\frac{3}{4}$ kg
	•		•	•	2$\frac{1}{4}$ kg
		•	•	•	1$\frac{3}{4}$ kg

Challenge   Encourage children to apply their listing skills in finding the 31 different vegetable boxes. Considering the empty box completes the symmetry of the pattern.

Number of vegetables in box	5	4	3	2	1	0
Number of ways	1	5	10	10	5	1

Coming together

- There are 5 possible 4-vegetable boxes. Encourage children to see that there are 5 blank spaces in the list, one for each vegetable.
- In the 3-vegetable boxes there are 6 entries and 4 blanks for each type of vegetable. Children who have not worked systematically can use this fact to check their list.

Taking it further
- Finding how many bags Lachie can make up from a 15 kg box of each type of vegetable.

Water carrier

Find different arrangements of bottles.

Resources

- 2 × 3 bottle carrier (such as supplied for wine by supermarkets)
- two identical plastic bottles
- enlarged Copymaster 28 (or OHT)
- Copymasters 28 and 29 for each child

Key vocabulary

litre, millilitre, arrangement, rectangle

Content

Arranging bottles in a 2 × 3 grid and calculating the total amount of liquid.

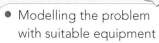

Communication
- Modelling the problem with suitable equipment
- Using a diagram to list possible arrangements

Reasoning
- Extending the problem to more bottles
- Using the information gathered

Decision-making
- Choosing method to record position of bottles in grid

Making a start

- Show the carrier and 1 bottle. Ask in how many different positions you can place the bottle in the carrier.
- Invite suggestions for ways of arranging 2 identical bottles in the carrier and allow children to model some of the possibilities. Discuss how the arrangements might be recorded. Establish that the 6 positions in the holder can be named, e.g. A to F, to avoid duplication.
- Display an enlarged Copymaster 28 and together record the 2-bottle arrangements suggested by shading the positions and writing the letters below.

Main activity

Core   Children find and record all the possible ways that 1 bottle and then 2 bottles can be arranged in the carrier.

Development Investigating ways that 3 bottles can be arranged in the carrier.

Challenge   Each bottle holds 750 ml. Children calculate the number of litres of water needed to make a display of carriers showing all the possible 2-bottle arrangements.

Coming together

- Invite children to explain how they used the grid to solve the problem for 2, then 3 bottles.
- Discuss listing strategies for checking that all the arrangements have been found.
- Ask children who completed the Challenge to explain their method of working out the answer.

Observing and supporting

Making a start

- To help children visualise a 'bird's eye view' of the carrier and hence a suitable recording diagram, hold up the empty carrier and show the vacant positions.

- Encourage the efficient use of positional language to describe 2-bottle arrangements, e.g. a bottle in the top right slot and a bottle in the middle left slot.

- Establish that since the bottles are identical, swapping over 2 bottles will give the same arrangement.

- To help children think of a simpler method for naming the 6 slots, you may want them to visualise a block of 6 flats/apartments, with 2 homes on the ground, middle and top floors. *How might the flats be named to help the postman deliver the mail?* (different numbers, letters)

- Label the slots in a 2 × 3 rectangular grid A to F. Ask the children to state the position of both bottles in each 2-bottle arrangement, e.g. AC, BD, AE …

A	B
C	D
E	F

Main activity

Core

Encourage children to start by finding all the possible positions for the second bottle when the first bottle is placed in slot A, i.e. AB, AC, AD, AE, AF. Then repeat with the first bottle in slot B, i.e. BC, BD, BE, BF. Remind children that BA would be the same as AB because the bottles are identical.

This gives 15 (5 + 4 + 3 + 2 + 1) possible arrangements of 2 bottles.

```
AB
AC   BC
AD   BD   CD
AE   BE   CE   DE
AF   BF   CF   DF   EF
```

Development

Establish a systematic way of finding 3-bottle arrangements. Encourage children to use their 2-bottle arrangements to help them. For example, suggest that children take each 2-bottle arrangement in turn and find all the possible positions for the third bottle. They should then check through to eliminate repeats. This gives 20 possible arrangements of 3 bottles.

Challenge

Encourage children to apply their knowledge of fractions to calculate the answer to 15 × 750 ml.
($15 \times \frac{3}{4}$ litres = $11\frac{1}{4}$ litres)

```
ABC
ABD
ABE
ABF
ACD   BCD
ACE   BCE
ACF   BCF
ADE   BDE   CDE
ADF   BDF   CDF
AEF   BEF   CEF   DEF
```

Coming together

- Stress that it is important to work systematically and make organised lists.

Taking it further

- Predicting the number of ways of placing 4, then 5, bottles in the carrier (15, 6) and explaining reasoning.

- Drawing a table to show the symmetry in the results.

Number of bottles	0	1	2	3	4	5	6
Number of ways	1	6	15	20	15	6	1

Slippery slugs

Find how long it takes a slug to crawl up the side of a garden tub to reach the juicy plants.

Resources

- metre stick and piece of Blu-tack for each group to represent tub and slug
- Copymaster 30 or squared paper for each child
- enlarged Copymaster 30 (or OHT)

Key vocabulary

metre, centimetre, distance, hour, minute, how long will it take to …?, vertical

Content

Calculating time taken.

Communication

- Explaining the problem in own words
- Drawing a diagram

Reasoning

- Applying rule to find slug's height after 20 minutes
- Predicting the time taken to complete the climb

Decision-making

- Checking results
- Choosing suitable scales for diagram

Making a start

- Display a sketch of a large garden tub and tell the story of a slug, which climbs up the outside of a shiny garden tub to reach the plants growing in it. Explain that the slug is so weak with hunger that it climbs for 10 minutes and rests for another 10 minutes. It takes the slug 10 minutes to climb 20 cm. However, as it rests, it slips 10 cm down the side of the tub. *How long will it take the slug to get to the top of the tub, which is 1 m high?*
- Invite children to retell story in their own words, describing the sides of the tub as e.g. shiny, slippery, upright, vertical.
- Ask how far the slug is from the ground at the end of 20 minutes and use suitable equipment to model and check the answer.
- Ask how far the slug has climbed in 60 minutes and discuss ways of recording the slug's progress over the hour. Show how this can be presented more clearly on a labelled grid, using an enlarged Copymaster 30 to model the process.
- Invite predictions for the time the slug takes to complete the climb.

Main activity

Core — Each group uses equipment to model the slug's climb to the top of the garden tub.

Development — Each child draws a record of the slug's climb.

Challenge — Finding the time it takes the slug to reach the top if it climbs 30 cm in 10 minutes then drops 10 cm in the next 10 minutes.

Coming together

- Invite children to explain how they used the equipment to solve the problem.
- Discuss the importance of checking answers with a suitable diagram.
- Use the children's responses to complete the diagram of the slug's progress on your enlarged Copymaster 30. Establish the slug's position at 60 and 120 minutes. Discuss why the final part of the climb was completed in less than 60 minutes.

Observing and supporting

 ## Making a start

- Encourage reasoned explanations such as: 'At the end of 20 minutes the slug is only 10 cm from the ground, because although it climbed 20 cm, it slipped down for 10 cm while it rested.'
- Discuss why a metre stick and some Blu-tack is a good choice of equipment to model the problem – the metre stick is the real height of the garden tub and is marked in multiples of 10 cm, and Blu-tack will stick to its surface but can be moved.
- Establish that because the slug's moves are vertical they are superimposed. Ask children to imagine that the lines of the moves are stretched out to the right, like a set of zigzag lines. Explain that we need to find a way to record the zigzag lines so that they show the height of each climb and slip and the time taken for each move. On the enlarged Copymaster 30, label the vertical axis in multiples of 10 cm and the horizontal axis in multiples of 10 minutes. Draw the zigzag lines to 20 minutes.

 ## Main activity

Core
Ask children to keep count of the time and record the slug's position every 10 minutes as they model its progress up the metre stick.

Development
Based on the rate of 30 cm in 60 minutes, children may predict that the slug will take more than 3 hours to reach the top of the garden tub. Encourage children to look for a pattern in their record of moves.

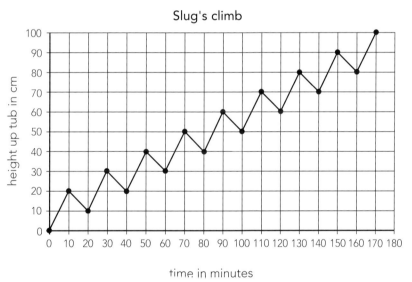

Challenge
The slug takes between 80 and 90 minutes. You may wish to ask children to find a way to refine their answer, assuming that the speed is constant while climbing. (86–87 minutes or $86\frac{2}{3}$ minutes)

 ## Coming together

- Stress the importance of checking answers and of using a suitable diagram to clarify the problem. The diagram helps children to see that the slug reaches the 1 m mark at 170 minutes and to reason that once there, it will not slip back.

Taking it further
- Making up a similar problem for a friend to solve, e.g. a koala bear climbing up a eucalyptus tree, a bottle being washed up the shoreline by the incoming tide …

Getting in shape

Make different shapes by joining two or three shapes.

Resources

- enlarged rectangles A and B from Copymaster 31
- enlarged square dot grid from Copymaster 31 (or OHT)
- Copymaster 31 for each child
- scissors for each child

Key vocabulary

triangle, square, rectangle, pentagon, hexagon, octagon, quadrilateral, right-angled, vertex, vertices, line of symmetry, investigate

Content

Naming shapes and identifying their properties.

Communication

- Naming and describing new shapes
- Drawing new shapes on square dot grid paper

Reasoning

- Finding new shapes by joining a triangle to shapes already found

Decision-making

- Deciding which shapes are duplicates
- Devising a method for recording shapes on square dot grid paper

Making a start

- Display the two rectangles cut out from an enlarged Copymaster 31. Ask children to close their eyes and visualise the two identical rectangles put together with sides touching to make a new shape. Elicit descriptions of the new shape then invite a child to make and name the one they have visualised. *Is this the only new shape we can make?*
- Discuss ways to record the new shapes on a square dot grid, and to show their properties.
- Cut along the dotted line of rectangle B and invite children to join rectangle A and one triangle along matching sides to make a new shape, and record it on the square dot grid.
- Discuss ways to eliminate duplicates.

Main activity

Core | Using Copymaster 31, children join one rectangle and one triangle along matching sides to make shapes with 4 sides, recording shapes on the square dot grid.

Development | Using the same rules for two triangles and one rectangle, children make and record as many different shapes as they can, marking equal sides, right angles and lines of symmetry in colour.

Challenge | Finding and sketching different shapes made by joining the two triangles along matching sides.

Coming together

- Using children's responses, record on your enlarged square dot grid a display of the new shapes made by putting together the two triangles and the rectangle.
- Together, name each shape and identify equal sides, right angles and lines of symmetry.
- Discuss strategies children used to find different shapes.

Observing and supporting

Making a start

- There are several possible combinations of the two rectangles, but only two are made by matching sides:

- Establish that the rectangle can be recorded on the grid as 2 units long and 1 unit wide.

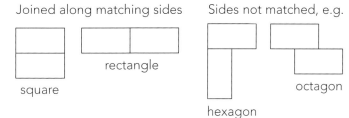

Joined along matching sides

square   rectangle

Sides not matched, e.g.

hexagon   octagon

- Discuss ways to record the properties of the shapes, such as marking equal sides (=), right angles (■) and lines of symmetry (---).

- Demonstrate that you have the same shape when it is rotated by 90°, 180° or 270°.

Main activity

Core
: Check that children record the two possible shapes correctly.

Development
: Ask children to find new shapes by joining a second triangle to each shape they made in the core activity, remembering to match equal sides. Solutions include:

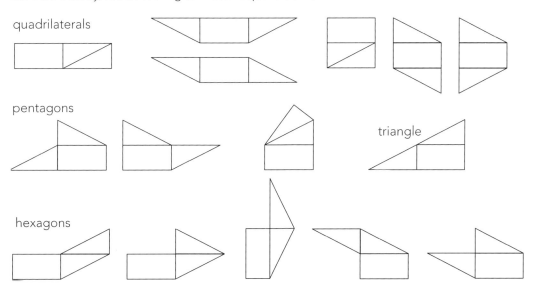

quadrilaterals

pentagons

triangle

hexagons

Challenge
: Encourage children to predict what shape is formed by flipping over one triangle and rejoining it to the second triangle along the same side.

Coming together

- Help children to identify and name irregular pentagons and hexagons by counting the number of sides.

Taking it further

- Dissecting a square into 3 pieces.
- Finding different shapes by joining 2 or 3 pieces.

Patterns with shapes

Use four small squares to make symmetrical patterns.

Resources

- multiple copies of set A squares from an enlarged Copymaster 32 (or OHT)
- Copymaster 32, scissors and mirror for each child
- Copymaster 33 for each child (plus some extra)
- backing paper and glue for the Challenge
- square grid or enlarged Copymaster 33 (or OHT) for the teacher

Key vocabulary

square, triangle, right-angled, mirror line, reflection, line of symmetry, symmetrical pattern, horizontal, vertical, diagonal, whole turn, half turn, quarter turn

Content

Identifying line symmetry in simple patterns, and recognising patterns with no line symmetry.

Communication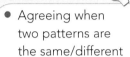
- Agreeing when two patterns are the same/different
- Drawing patterns

Reasoning
- Looking for all possible patterns with line symmetry
- Testing patterns for line symmetry

Decision-making
- Checking for duplication of patterns

Making a start

- Display the half-coloured squares from set A of an enlarged Copymaster 32 and invite children to use the four squares to make a pattern in a 4 × 1 rectangular arrangement.
- Establish when two patterns are the same/different.
- Discuss which patterns have line symmetry.
- Invite suggestions of what children could try next. Ask them to fit the four small squares into a large 2 × 2 square to make a pattern. Discuss strategies for recording patterns.

Main activity

Core	Children use the four half-coloured squares from set A to make different 2 × 2 square patterns.
Development	Finding as many different 2 × 2 square patterns as possible using the four half-coloured squares from set A. Identifying those that have line symmetry.
Challenge	Using the squares with black and white isosceles triangles from sets B and C to explore patterns in a 2 × 2 square.

Coming together

- Collect 2 × 2 square patterns made from set A and draw them on your square grid or an enlarged Copymaster 33.
- Ask which patterns are symmetrical. Identify patterns that have more than one line of symmetry.
- Choose two patterns and ask children to describe how they are similar/different.
- Discuss the display of 2 × 2 squares made by the Challenge group, focusing on line symmetry, similarities and differences.

Observing and supporting

Making a start

- You may wish to letter the squares in the rectangular arrangement **a** to **d**:
- Encourage children to find symmetrical arrangements by making quarter and half turns of the small squares. Elicit that the square in **a** is reflected in **d** and the square in **b** is reflected in **c**. Establish that rotations represent the same pattern arrangement; for example,

| a | b | c | d |

 is the same as

- For a 4 × 1 rectangular arrangement, there are eight patterns with line symmetry:

  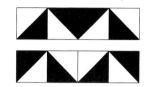 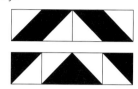

- Show the pattern on the right and discuss ways in which it might be recorded. Distribute Copymaster 33 and explain that we can make a neat and accurate drawing by drawing in the diagonals of the small squares.

Main activity

Core Establish that you have the same pattern when a 2 × 2 arrangement is rotated.

Development Remind children to use their mirrors when checking for symmetry. There are 16 2 × 2 square patterns with line symmetry. Patterns **a** and **b** have 4 lines of symmetry, patterns **f** and **o** have 2 lines of symmetry, while the remaining patterns have just 1 line of symmetry:

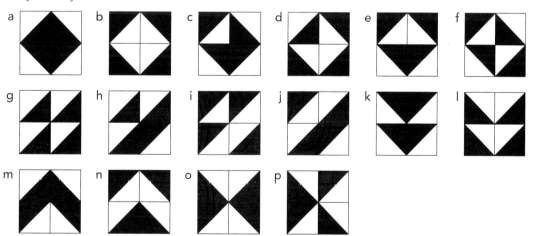

Challenge Encourage children to explore patterns that use two squares from set B and two squares from set C. Mount a group display on backing paper.

Coming together

- Encourage the use of precise mathematical vocabulary when children explain the similarities and differences between two patterns.

Taking it further

- Exploring symmetrical patterns made with small squares in a 4 × 2 rectangle.

Take your seat

Find seat numbers for passengers so that families can sit together.

Resources

- twelve pupil chairs
- seven large cards labelled A, B, C, D, 1, 2, 3
- six blank cards
- enlarged Copymaster 34 (or OHT)
- Copymaster 34 for each child
- Copymasters 35 and 36 for each pair for the Challenge
- scissors for each pair

Key vocabulary

grid, row, column, between, beside, in front, behind, middle, next to, across, aisle

Content

Describing and finding the position of a square on a grid with labelled rows and columns.

Communication

- Using positional language to describe the location of a square
- Recording seat numbers in a table

Reasoning

- Organising seating arrangements according to given criteria

Decision-making

- Checking that results answer the question

Making a start

- Explain that 12 children are taking the school mini-bus to the Sports Centre. Arrange 12 pupil chairs in 3 rows of 4 with an aisle between columns B and C.

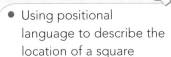

- Invite 6 children to distribute themselves over the 12 bus seats.
- Establish which children have window or aisle seats.
- Discuss the use of a grid system to describe the position of each bus seat and place cards on the floor to show rows 1 to 3 and columns A to D.
- Establish the number of an empty seat, e.g. B2, write it on a blank card and give the card to a child who takes that seat on the bus. Continue to fill the remaining seats.
- Display an enlarged Copymaster 34 showing an aircraft seating plan. Discuss the problem of allocating seats to the remaining passengers so that their requirements (shown on the name cards) can all be met.

Main activity

Core   Children work in groups to find seats for the remaining passengers so that families can sit together.

Development   Recording where passengers are seated.

Challenge   Working in pairs, children explore ways of allocating a new block of 25 seats so that families can sit together for the return journey, using Copymasters 35 and 36.

Coming together

- Invite children to complete the seating plan for the passengers on the outward journey on your enlarged Copymaster 34. Check that all passenger requirements have been met.

Observing and supporting

Making a start

- You may wish to adopt this routine: 'Enter the bus from the door in front of seat D1, walk across, then up the aisle if your seat is in rows 2 or 3.'
- Revise positional language by asking children to describe a chosen seat, e.g. 'Becky has an aisle seat in the same row as … next to … between ….'
- The strategy of acting out the situation can help children relate the practical, 'real-life' activity to the more abstract but similar task of allocating aircraft seats in the main activity. Explain that some seats have already been reserved for other passengers.

Main activity

Core Check that children can interpret the plan. *Which letters show a window seat?* (A, E) … *an aisle seat?* (B, C)

Development You may wish to suggest that children write seat numbers in pencil on the cards so that they can make changes, if necessary. Stress the importance of writing the letter followed by the number for a seat, e.g. B3. A possible seating arrangement is:

	A	B	C	D	E
row 5	Reserved	Mr Amber	Mrs Amber		Reserved
row 4	Bill Black	Liz Black	Reserved	Reserved	
row 3	Debbie Green	Mrs Green	Mr Green	Darren Green	
row 2	Trish Ruby	Mel Ruby	Reserved		Reserved
row 1		Reserved	Mr Brown	Mrs Brown	Jamie Brown

Challenge A possible seating arrangement is:

	A	B	C	D	E
row 5		Mr Amber	Mrs Amber	Liz Black	Bill Black
row 4	Cora Whyte	Mrs Whyte	Mr Whyte	Steve Whyte	Alan Whyte
row 3	Debbie Green	Mrs Green	Mr Green	Darren Green	
row 2	Rob Collora	Mrs Collora	Mr Collora	Kev Collora	Kim Collora
row 1	Trish Ruby	Mel Ruby	Mr Brown	Mrs Brown	Jamie Brown

Coming together

- Establish that the four Greens will need row 3, that the Browns will take seats C1 (Mr B), D1 (Mrs B) and E1 (Jamie), and that the Ambers have seats B5 and C5. Check that children give the letter first when saying a seat allocation.

Taking it further

- Investigating seating plans for other aircraft with different seating arrangements.

Program patterns

Make patterns by repeating right-angled turns.

Resources

- counter and blindfold
- Copymaster 37 for each child
- supply of 1 cm squared paper for the Challenge
- enlarged squared grid (or OHT) for the teacher

Key vocabulary

direction, route, clockwise, anticlockwise, quarter turn, right angle, vertex, program

Content

Using a program to create patterns using clockwise right-angled turns.

Communication
- Explaining how the pattern works
- Drawing patterns

Reasoning
- Considering why a program with three different forward steps produces a pattern that returns to the starting point

Decision-making
- Checking results

Making a start

- Make some open floor space. Blindfold a child and place a counter on the floor at their feet. Ask the child to imagine they are a robot and to follow these instructions: *Walk forward three steps, make a quarter turn clockwise.* Repeat the instructions *three* more times (i.e. a total of *four* times).
- Discuss the route traced out on the floor by the 'robot'.
- Explain that a robot can only follow instructions. We have to tell it what to do. We write the instructions as a program.
- Establish the program for walking out a square as ' FD 3 RT 90 REPEAT 4 END'.
- Write up: FD 2 RT 90 FD 1 RT 90 FD 3 RT 90. Ask children to imagine a robot following these instructions and to draw the route it takes 'in the air'.
- Discuss why squared paper is suitable for recording the route.

Main activity

Core
Children record the path of the robot following the route
FD 2 RT 90 FD 1 RT 90 FD 3 RT 90 REPEAT 4 END (program 1).

Development
Drawing two further repeating programs:
FD 3 RT 90 FD 2 RT 90 FD 4 RT 90 REPEAT 4 END (program 2)
FD 3 RT 90 FD 5 RT 90 FD 7 RT 90 REPEAT 4 END (program 3)

Challenge
Investigating patterns, continuing as far as possible:
FD 1 RT 90 FD 2 RT 90 FD 3 RT 90 FD 4 RT 90 REPEAT (program 4)
FD 3 RT 90 FD 1 RT 90 FD 2 RT 90 FD 4 RT 90 REPEAT (program 5)

Coming together

- Draw the completed pattern from the core activity (program 1) on a square grid. Discuss children's ideas as to why the pattern returns to the starting point.
- Discuss similarities and differences between the three patterns in the core and development activities.
- Display, then discuss, some of the repeating patterns made in the challenge activity.

Observing and supporting

Making a start

- You may wish to introduce the problem by discussing the use of robots in industry.
- Establish that the 'robot' walks out a square with sides 3 steps long, makes a right-angled turn at each vertex and returns to the starting point. (You may wish to explain that a right angle is 90°.)
- Explain that we use a special program to instruct the robot:

Program	What the robot does
FD 3	walks forward 3 steps
RT 90	makes a right turn through one right angle
REPEAT 4	walks forward and turns right 4 times in total
END	stops after the 4th time

- Draw this route on a squared grid and ask children to copy it on Copymaster 37.
Explain that if we want the robot to walk the route four times then we write this program for it:
FD 2 RT 90 FD 1 RT 90 FD 3 RT 90 REPEAT 4 END

Route
FD 2 RT 90
FD 1 RT 90
FD 3 RT 90

Main activity

Core   Some children may have difficulty in distinguishing between right and left turns. Ensure they draw the first line going up their squared paper. Suggest they then rotate the paper so that each subsequent line in turn faces upwards.

FD 2 RT 90
FD 1 RT 90
FD 3 RT 90
FD 3 RT 90
REPEAT 4
END

1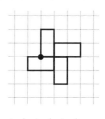

Development   Check that children's patterns form a closed shape by returning to the starting point.

2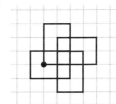

3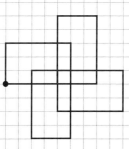

Challenge   If time permits, encourage children to explore patterns made by different combinations of the forward steps.

4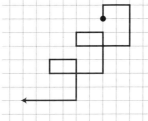

5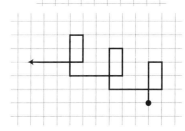

Coming together

- Recall that four quarter turns in the same direction make one complete turn. Making a series of forward steps and quarter turns clockwise will lead to some kind of spiralling pattern.
- In the core and development activities, with only three different forward steps, a closed shape is formed.
- Where there are four different forward steps, the pattern is open.

Taking it further
- Investigating computer programs using LOGO.

Dolly Mixture

Analyse the contents of a bag of sweets.

Resources

- large sheet of sugar paper
- packet of Dolly Mixture (or similar sweet mix) for each group plus a packet for the teacher
- Copymaster 38 or squared paper for each child

Key vocabulary

count, tally, sort, frequency table, bar chart, most/least common, predict

Content

Collecting, sorting, organising and displaying information.

Communication

- Discussing contents of bag and tally chart

Reasoning

- Predicting the contents of a second bag
- Explaining significance of results
- Organising a frequency table

Decision-making

- Choosing categories for sorting contents
- Choosing ways to represent results graphically

Making a start

- Pour the contents of a Dolly Mixture bag onto a large piece of sugar paper and ask for ways of sorting the sweets. List the categories of sweets agreed, such as 'round pink' or 'square orange'.
- Discuss ways of recording how many of each type there are (the frequency). You may want to focus on a few types to begin with. Ask questions that use the vocabulary of data handling: *What does the tally chart show? Which type is the most common/least common?*
- Show another, unopened, packet of Dolly Mixture. Ask children if this packet will have the same number of each type. Encourage debate about this and ask children to justify their predictions.
- Give each group a packet of Dolly Mixture to investigate. Ask them to record a prediction of the contents of their packet.

Main activity

Core	Each group records the content of their own packet and creates a frequency table.
Development	Children draw a bar chart of the final tally.
Challenge	Drawing a bar chart of the contents of the original demonstration packet and comparing this with their chart for their own packet.

Coming together

- Ask each group to describe what they did and found out. Establish whether all the packets had the same number of each type of sweet and discuss how accurate the predictions were.
- Choose two or three of the sweet types and collate the results of all the groups in a table. *How similar were the results?*

Observing and supporting

Making a start

- Typical ways of sorting sweets are by colour, shape or size and, in some cases, a combination of these.
- Model the tallying – four strokes down and a fifth across. A typical error is to make five downward tallies then one across, thus counting six objects as a group of five. When the tallying is complete show children how to count in fives to find the total. An example tally chart is shown here.

Type	Tally	Total
pink round	++++ ++++		11
brown cubes	||||	4
yellow sugary	++++ ||	7

- The debate about whether or not a second packet will have the same contents is important because it provides the incentive for accurate tallying in the main activity.

Main activity

Core: Check strategies for tallying – children may find it easier to sort the sweets into different types before tallying. Ask questions that encourage children to compare their result with their prediction.

Development: Since the items are discrete there should be a gap between the bars on the bar chart. Copymaster 38 provides a framework for drawing the bar chart.

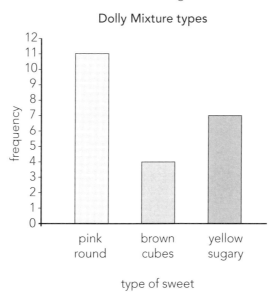

Dolly Mixture types

Challenge: In order to make a comparison it is important to draw both charts with the bars in the same order.

Coming together

- Children should be given the opportunity to discuss their findings and reflect on how they have worked. Help children articulate by pointing out things you noticed as they were working. Focus the discussion on the way they have collected and represented the data.
- Discuss why no two packets of Dolly Mixture are identical and why some sweet types are less common than others.

Taking it further

- Using computer graph-drawing software to generate further graphs.

Bedtime

Investigate what time children go to bed.

Resources

- enlarged Copymaster 39 (or OHT)
- two copies of Copymaster 40 or squared paper for each child

Key vocabulary

count, tally, frequency, frequency table, graph, axis, axes, bar chart, most/least common, label, title

Content

Organising and displaying information.

Communication
- Discussing table of information

Reasoning
- Predicting what will be the most/least common bedtimes
- Looking for a pattern in the bar charts

Decision-making
- Choosing methods for tallying
- Choosing ways to represent results graphically

Making a start

- Discuss the bedtimes of children in the class. *Are these the same during the week and at the weekend?* Encourage children to give times to the nearest half hour (which often coincides with the end of a particular TV programme!).
- Display an enlarged Copymaster 39. Explain that it shows information about the bedtimes of 24 Year 3 pupils at Hutford Primary School.
- Ask questions about the data: *What is the earliest weekday/weekend bedtime? … the latest? … most/least common?*
- Discuss ways of recording how many children went to bed at different times. Choose one method and complete it on the board for both weekdays and the weekend.

Main activity

Core	Children draw a bar chart of weekday bedtimes.
Development	Drawing a bar chart of weekend bedtimes. In small groups children compare the two charts.
Challenge	Comparing bedtimes of boys and girls during the week and at weekends.

Coming together

- Discuss the weekday and weekend bar charts, establishing their similarities and differences. Draw attention to the shapes of the two graphs.
- Discuss how the bar charts enable us to answer questions such as: *Which is the most common/least common bedtime? Are there any bedtimes that have the same frequency? How many more children go to bed at 'time A' than 'time B'?*

Observing and supporting

Making a start

- It is important to make sure children understand how the table works. Ask questions such as: *What time does Julie go to bed at the weekend? Which two boys go to bed at 7 o'clock during the week?*
- Suggest appropriate methods of recording if necessary and model the tallying. The bedtimes for weekdays and weekends should be tallied separately in order for a comparison to be made:

Weekday bedtimes

Bedtimes	Tally	Frequency
7:00	||	2
7:30	⧗⧗⧗	5
8:00	⧗⧗⧗ ⧗⧗⧗ |	11
8:30	⧗⧗⧗	5
9:00	|	1

Weekend bedtimes

Bedtimes	Tally	Frequency
8:30	|	1
9:00	|||	3
9:30	⧗⧗⧗	5
10:00	⧗⧗⧗ ||	7
10:30	⧗⧗⧗ |||	8

- Relate the terms most common and least common to the highest and lowest values in the frequency tables.

Main activity

Core
Remind children to label the axes and include a title. Frequencies should be marked on the vertical axis; suggest one square for each person. Bedtimes should be marked on the horizontal axis and, since time is a continuous measure, the bars should be touching. Copymaster 40 provides a framework for drawing the bar charts.

Development
Ask children to compare the shapes of their graphs, which should look like this:

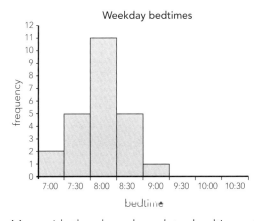

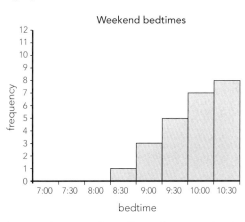

Challenge
More girls than boys have later bedtimes. This can be seen by tallying boys and girls separately or by colouring different sections of the bars to represent boys and girls. For example, for weekday bedtimes of 8:00 colour the bottom four squares blue (since four boys have that bedtime) and the rest green (since seven girls have that bedtime).

Coming together

- Children should notice that the weekday bedtime information produces a 'normal distribution' shape, peaking in the centre, whereas the weekend bedtime is skewed towards the later time (presumably because more children are able to convince parents to let them stay up later at weekends).

Taking it further
- Conducting your own class survey of bedtimes.

Bags of cubes

Investigate the different numbers of coloured cubes in a bag.

Resources

- initial pair of bags labelled A and B, one with 5 red and 5 green cubes, one with 2 red and 8 green
- six further pairs of bags labelled A and B, two pairs each of the following sets:

  SET 1: Bag A – 7 red, 3 green cubes; Bag B – 3 red, 7 green cubes.

  SET 2: Bag A – 6 red, 4 green cubes; Bag B – 9 red, 1 green cube.

  SET 3: Bag A – 6 red, 4 green cubes; Bag B – 4 red, 6 green cubes.

- several copies of Copymaster 41 appropriately labelled for use with each set
- enlarged Copymaster 41 (or OHT)

Key vocabulary

most/least common, predict, investigate

Content

Collecting, recording and interpreting information.

Communication

- Recording results in a table
- Explaining results

Reasoning

- Predicting based upon evidence
- Justifying predictions

Decision-making

- Deciding the number of trials needed before making a prediction

Making a start

- Show children the initial two bags of cubes without showing the contents. Tell them that one bag has two red and eight green cubes, and the other has five red and five green cubes. Display an enlarged Copymaster 41.
- Start with Bag A. Ask a child to pull out one cube, show everyone, then put it back and shake the bag. On the Copymaster, tick red or green for draw 1 of Bag A. Repeat the procedure for a cube from Bag B.
- After five draws from each bag, ask children to predict which bag is which and record the predicted numbers of cubes on the Copymaster.
- Continue drawing cubes from alternate bags, stopping after 10 and 15 draws to make further predictions. After 20 draws record a final prediction then check the contents of each bag.

Main activity

Core   In six small groups children repeat the investigation using a new pair of bags. Tell children how many cubes the bags contain, but not which is which. This information should be written on each group's copy of Copymaster 41.

Development   Investigating a further pair of bags.

Challenge   Investigating a bag without being told anything about the colours of the 10 cubes inside.

Coming together

- One child from each group reports on their investigation, in particular how difficult it was to predict at each stage.

Observing and supporting

Making a start

- In almost every case there will be more green cubes pulled from the bag with 2 red and 8 green (there is a four in five chance of getting a green) than in the bag with 5 red and 5 green (where there is a one in two chance of getting a green).
- Children should see that the greater incidence of green cubes is the clue to the prediction.
- It is theoretically possible that in any particular experiment more green cubes might be drawn from the bag with 5 red and 5 green, although increasing the number of draws should make the trends clearer. This is the reason for stopping after each group of five draws to review the predictions.

Main activity

Core | Stress the importance of returning the cube to the bag before redrawing (and no peeking!). Encourage group discussion before each prediction, which should be focused on the evidence from the draws.

Development | Children should compare their two investigations: *Was one easier to predict than the other?*

Challenge | Without any clues as to the content of the bag children need to compare very carefully the numbers of each colour drawn.

Coming together

- Encourage children to discuss their predictions, justifying them on the basis of the evidence. Ask questions to encourage this discussion: *Which were easy to predict? Which harder? Who was sure, who unsure about their predictions? Did the whole group agree? Could you tell before all 20 draws were complete?*
- Compare completed Copymasters from different groups who had the same pairs of bags. *Why are the results different? What would happen if you repeated the investigation?* At this level it is sufficient for children to see that what happens will be different each time, and the numbers of each colour in the bags mean that over time trends can be observed upon which predictions can be made.
- For any particular pair of bags you might want to pool all of the results.

Taking it further

- Investigating two bags of 20 cubes with three different colours.

Long distance runners (1)

Names:

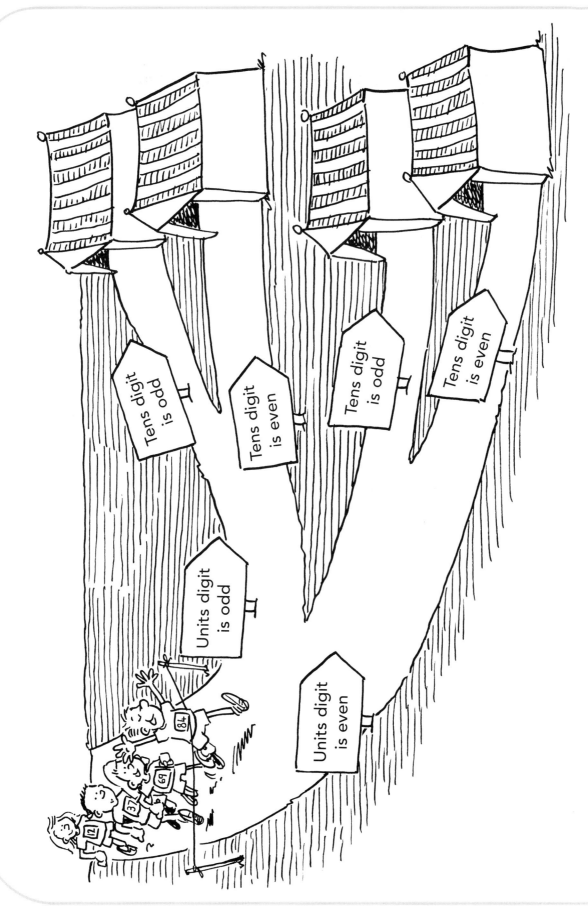

Long distance runners (2)

Names:

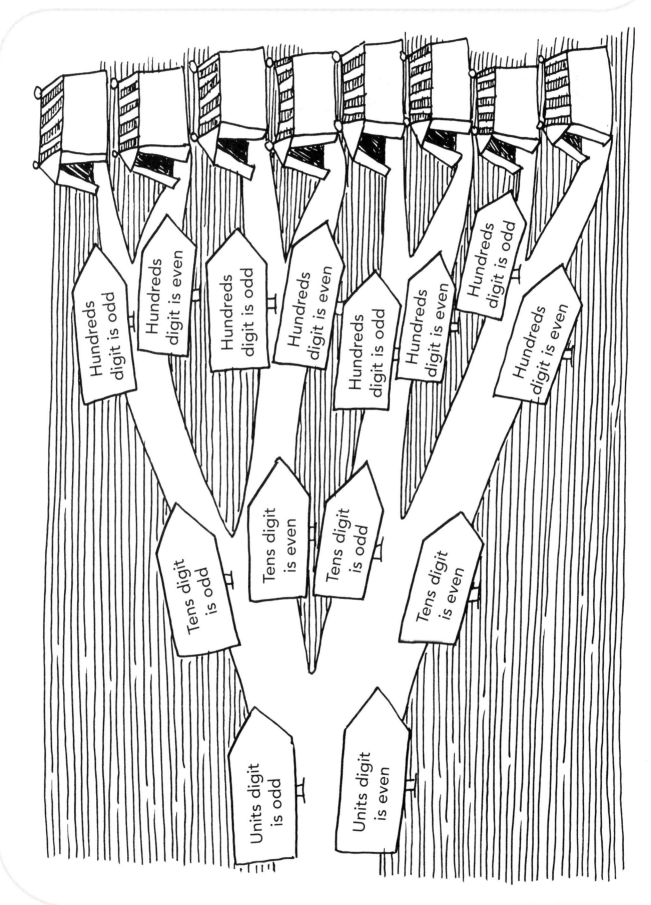

Charity envelopes

Name:

House number	Adam (multiples of 2)	Bess (multiples of 5)	Chloe (multiples of 10)	

Loading parcels (1)

Loading parcels (2)

Jumping frogs (1)

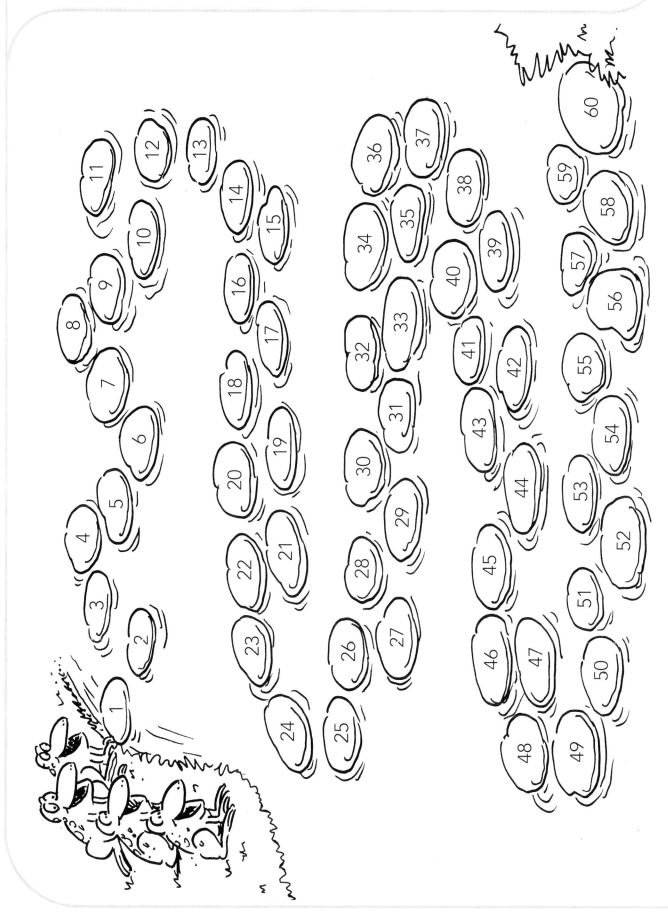

Jumping frogs (2)

Name:

Stone	Twody (jumps in 2s)	Threedy (jumps in 3s)	Fourdy (jumps in 4s)	Fivedy (jumps in 5s)	Total number of frogs landing

Where will I sleep?

Name:

First number ...			
... is 1	... is 2	... is 3	... is 4

From post to post (1)

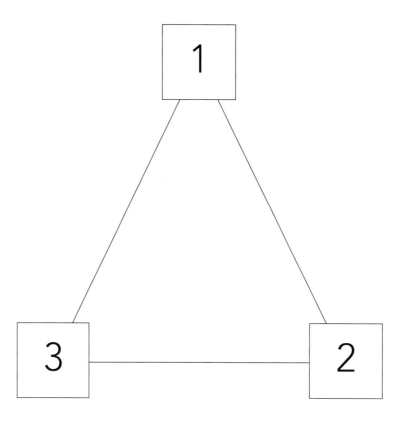

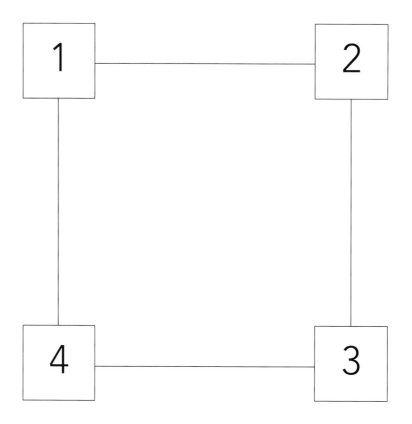

From post to post (2)

Name:

Start on ☐ and count on ☐ _____

☐ → ☐ → ☐ → ☐ → ☐ → ☐ → ☐ → ☐ → ☐

Start on ☐ and count on ☐ _____

☐ → ☐ → ☐ → ☐ → ☐ → ☐ → ☐ → ☐ → ☐

Start on ☐ and count on ☐ _____

☐ → ☐ → ☐ → ☐ → ☐ → ☐ → ☐ → ☐ → ☐

Start on ☐ and count on ☐ _____

☐ → ☐ → ☐ → ☐ → ☐ → ☐ → ☐ → ☐ → ☐

Start on ☐ and count on ☐ _____

☐ → ☐ → ☐ → ☐ → ☐ → ☐ → ☐ → ☐ → ☐

Start on ☐ and count on ☐ _____

☐ → ☐ → ☐ → ☐ → ☐ → ☐ → ☐ → ☐ → ☐

Can you halve it?

Name:

Object	How we halved it	How accurate we were
string		
apple		
sweets		

Speedy deliveries (1)

Name:

Total	Stamps needed
10p	
11p	
12p	
13p	
14p	
15p	
16p	
17p	
18p	
19p	
20p	

Speedy deliveries (2)

2p	2p	2p	2p	2p
2p	2p	2p	2p	2p
4p	4p	4p	4p	4p
4p	4p	4p	4p	4p

Lucky dice

Name:

	Second dice is a 1	Second dice is a 2	Second dice is a 3	Second dice is a 4	Second dice is a 5	Second dice is a 6
First dice is 1	$1 + 1 = 2$	$1 + 2 = 3$	$1 + 3 = 4$			
First dice is 2	$2 + 1 = 3$		$2 + 3 = 5$			
First dice is 3		$3 + 2 = 5$		$3 + 4 = 7$	$3 + 5 = 8$	
First dice is 4	$4 + 1 = 5$					$4 + 6 = 10$
First dice is 5			$5 + 3 = 8$			
First dice is 6						$6 + 6 = 12$

Short Jack's silver

Moving tiger cubs

Take-away (1)

MENU

Soup
Chicken and sweetcorn £1·10

Mushroom £1·00

Minced beef £1·20

Appetisers
Spare ribs £1·60

Prawn toast £1·50

Spring roll £1·20

Side orders
Prawn crackers 70p

Mixed vegetables £1·10

Noodles 90p

Rice dishes
Fried rice £1·10

Roast pork fried rice £1·30

Special fried rice £1·20

Chicken dishes
Chicken and pineapple £2·30

Chicken and vegetables £2·10

Chicken and green pepper £2·40

King prawn dishes
King prawn with beansprouts £2·50

King prawn with ginger £2·40

King prawn with oyster sauce £2·40

Vegetarian dishes
Mushroom Chop Suey £2·40

Vegetable Foo Yung £2·20

Mixed vegetable Chow Mein £2·50

Desserts
Banana fritter £1·00

Pineapple fritter £1·00

Ice cream 80p

Take-away (2)

Names:

Meal	Starter	Main course	Rice	Side order	Dessert	Total cost
1						
2						
3						
4						

Bus riders

Name:

There are ☐ fewer people each day.

	Monday	Tuesday	Wednesday	Thursday	Friday	Total
1st try						
2nd try						
3rd try						
4th try						
5th try						
6th try						
7th try						
8th try						
9th try						
10th try						
11th try						
12th try						
13th try						
14th try						
15th try						

On target

Name:

1st beanbag is a 2	1st beanbag is a 3	1st beanbag is a 5	1st beanbag is a 10

Join-ups (1)

Names:

Measuring	Working out

Length of strips in cm		
Red (R)	Blue (B)	White (W)

Length of strips in cm		
Total of R + B + W	$\frac{1}{2}$ of total	$\frac{1}{2}$ of total minus R

Join-ups (2)

Measure each strip to the nearest half centimetre.

Write the length on each one and cut it out.

R1 _____ cm

R2 _____ cm

R3 _____ cm

R4 _____ cm

- -

Measure each strip to the nearest half centimetre.

Write the length on each one and cut it out.

R1 _____ cm

R2 _____ cm

R3 _____ cm

R4 _____ cm

Measure each strip to the nearest half centimetre.

Write the length on each one and cut it out.

B1 _____ cm

B2 _____ cm

B3 _____ cm

B4 _____ cm

- -

Measure each strip to the nearest half centimetre.

Write the length on each one and cut it out.

B1 _____ cm

B2 _____ cm

B3 _____ cm

B4 _____ cm

Measure the strips to the nearest half centimetre.

Write the length on each one and cut it out.

W1 _____ cm

W2 _____ cm

W3 _____ cm

W4 _____ cm

Measure the strips to the nearest half centimetre.

Write the length on each one and cut it out.

W1 _____ cm

W2 _____ cm

W3 _____ cm

W4 _____ cm

Filling the space (1)

Name:

Gap	How lengths are used
5 cm	
6 cm	
7 cm	
8 cm	
9 cm	
10 cm	
11 cm	
12 cm	

Filling the space (2)

Name:

Length of gap	How lengths are used
13 cm	
15 cm	
17 cm	
19 cm	
21 cm	
23 cm	
25 cm	
27 cm	
29 cm	

Length of gap	How lengths are used
12 cm	
14 cm	
16 cm	
18 cm	
20 cm	
22 cm	
24 cm	
26 cm	
28 cm	

Vegetable boxes

Name:

Highland Organic Farm

Bag of potatoes	Bag of carrots	Bag of leeks	Bag of onions	Bag of mushrooms	Total weight

Water carrier (1)

Name:

1 bottle

A	B
C	D
E	F

A	B
C	D
E	F

A	B
C	D
E	F

A	B
C	D
E	F

A	B
C	D
E	F

A	B
C	D
E	F

_____ _____ _____ _____ _____ _____

2 bottles

A	B
C	D
E	F

A	B
C	D
E	F

A	B
C	D
E	F

A	B
C	D
E	F

A	B
C	D
E	F

_____ _____ _____ _____ _____

A	B
C	D
E	F

A	B
C	D
E	F

A	B
C	D
E	F

A	B
C	D
E	F

A	B
C	D
E	F

_____ _____ _____ _____ _____

A	B
C	D
E	F

A	B
C	D
E	F

A	B
C	D
E	F

A	B
C	D
E	F

A	B
C	D
E	F

_____ _____ _____ _____ _____

Water carrier (2)

Name:

3 bottles

A	B
C	D
E	F

A	B
C	D
E	F

A	B
C	D
E	F

A	B
C	D
E	F

A	B
C	D
E	F

A	B
C	D
E	F

A	B
C	D
E	F

A	B
C	D
E	F

A	B
C	D
E	F

A	B
C	D
E	F

A	B
C	D
E	F

A	B
C	D
E	F

A	B
C	D
E	F

A	B
C	D
E	F

A	B
C	D
E	F

A	B
C	D
E	F

A	B
C	D
E	F

A	B
C	D
E	F

A	B
C	D
E	F

A	B
C	D
E	F

Slippery slugs

Name:

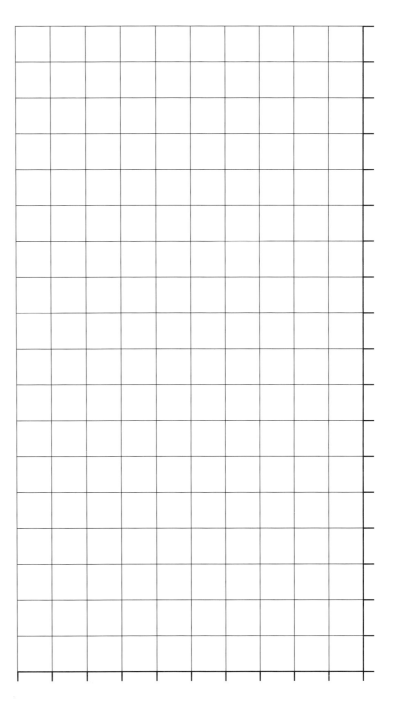

Slug's climb

time in minutes

height of tub in cm

Getting in shape

Name:

A

B

Patterns with shapes (1)

Cut out the four squares in Set A.

Place them in this large square and make a pattern.

Copy your pattern onto Copymaster 33.

Now make another pattern.

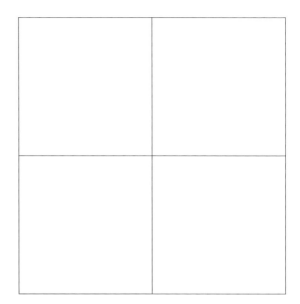

Set A

Set B

Set C

   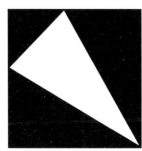

Patterns with shapes (2)

Name:

Take your seat (1)

Name:

	A	B		C	D	E
Row 5	Reserved					Reserved
Row 4				Reserved	Reserved	
Row 3						
Row 2				Reserved		Reserved
Row 1		Reserved				

Aircraft aisle

Cut out the name cards:

Mr Green aisle seat	Mrs Green seat	Debbie Green window seat	Darren Green next to dad seat	Bill Black window seat	Liz Black seat ....
Mrs Brown seat	Jamie Brown window seat	Mr Brown aisle seat	Mr Amber aisle – same row as Mrs A seat	Mrs Amber aisle – same row as Mr A seat	Mel Ruby aisle seat	Trish Ruby seat ....

Take your seat (2)

Names:

| | Row 5 | | | | | |
| Row 5 | | | | | | |

Aircraft aisle

Row 5

Row 4

Row 3

Row 2

Row 1

| A | B | C | D | E |

Name	Seat	Name	Seat	Name	Seat

Take your seat (3)

Mr Green	Mrs Green	Darren Green
aisle	seat	next to dad
seat		seat ....
		Debbie Green
		window
		seat ....

Mel Ruby	Trish Ruby	Mrs Amber
aisle	seat	aisle – same row as Mr A
seat		seat ....
		Mr Amber
		aisle – same row as Mrs A
		seat ....

Bill Black	Liz Black	Cora Whyte
window	seat	next to mum
seat		seat ....
		Mrs Whyte
		seat ....

Alan Whyte	Steve Whyte	Kev Collora
window	next to brother	between Kim and dad
seat	seat	seat ....
		Mr Whyte
		seat ....

Rob Collora	Mrs Collora	Kim Collora
window	seat	seat ....
seat		Mr Collora
		seat ....

Mrs Brown	Jamie Brown	Mr Brown
seat	window	aisle
	seat	seat ....

Mr Green	Mrs Green	Darren Green
aisle	seat	next to dad
seat		seat ....
		Debbie Green
		window
		seat ....

Mel Ruby	Trish Ruby	Mrs Amber
aisle	seat	aisle – same row as Mr A
seat		seat ....
		Mr Amber
		aisle – same row as Mrs A
		seat ....

Bill Black	Liz Black	Cora Whyte
window	seat	next to mum
seat		seat ....
		Mrs Whyte
		seat ....

Alan Whyte	Steve Whyte	Kev Collora
window	next to brother	between Kim and dad
seat	seat	seat ....
		Mr Whyte
		seat ....

Rob Collora	Mrs Collora	Kim Collora
window	seat	seat ....
seat		Mr Collora
		seat ....

Mrs Brown	Jamie Brown	Mr Brown
seat	window	aisle
	seat	seat ....

Program patterns

Name:

Program 1
FD 2 RT 90
FD 1 RT 90
FD 3 RT 90
REPEAT 4
END

Program 2
FD 3 RT 90
FD 2 RT 90
FD 4 RT 90
REPEAT 4
END

Program 3
FD 3 RT 90
FD 5 RT 90
FD 7 RT 90
REPEAT 4
END

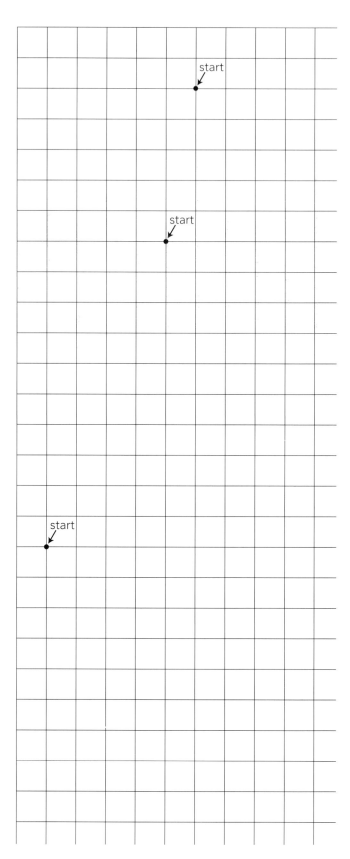

start

start

start

Dolly Mixture

Name:

Dolly Mixture types

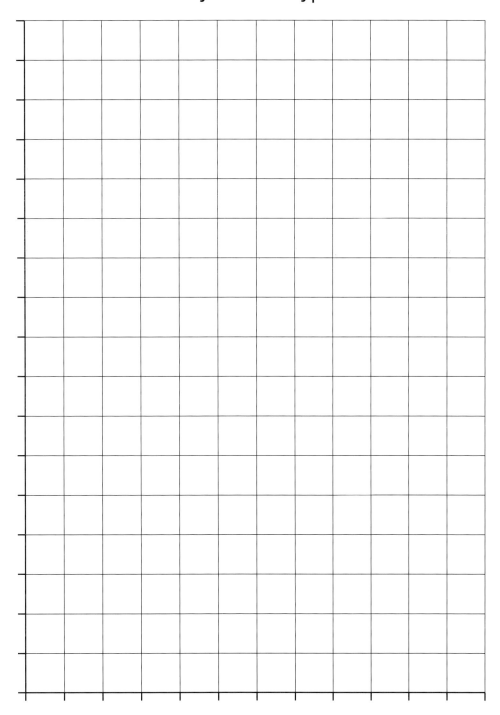

frequency

type of sweet

Bedtime (1)

Hutford Primary School – Class 3G bedtimes

	Boy or girl?	Weekdays	Weekends
Peter	B	7:00	9:30
Andrew	B	8:00	8:30
Hussain	B	8:00	9:00
Matthew	B	8:30	10:00
Vladimir	B	7:30	9:30
Scott	B	7:30	10:00
John	B	8:30	10:30
Jamie	B	8:00	10:30
Clive	B	7:30	9:30
Pierre	B	7:00	10:30
Sean	B	7:30	9:30
Roger	B	8:00	10:00
Stephanie	G	8:00	10:30
Julie	G	7:30	10:00
Nadia	G	8:00	9:00
Angela	G	9:00	9:00
Petra	G	8:00	10:00
Siobhan	G	8:30	10:00
Anita	G	8:00	9:30
Samia	G	8:00	10:30
Marge	G	8:00	10:30
Lydia	G	8:30	10:00
Patricia	G	8:30	10:30
Constance	G	8:00	10:30

Bedtime (2)

Name:

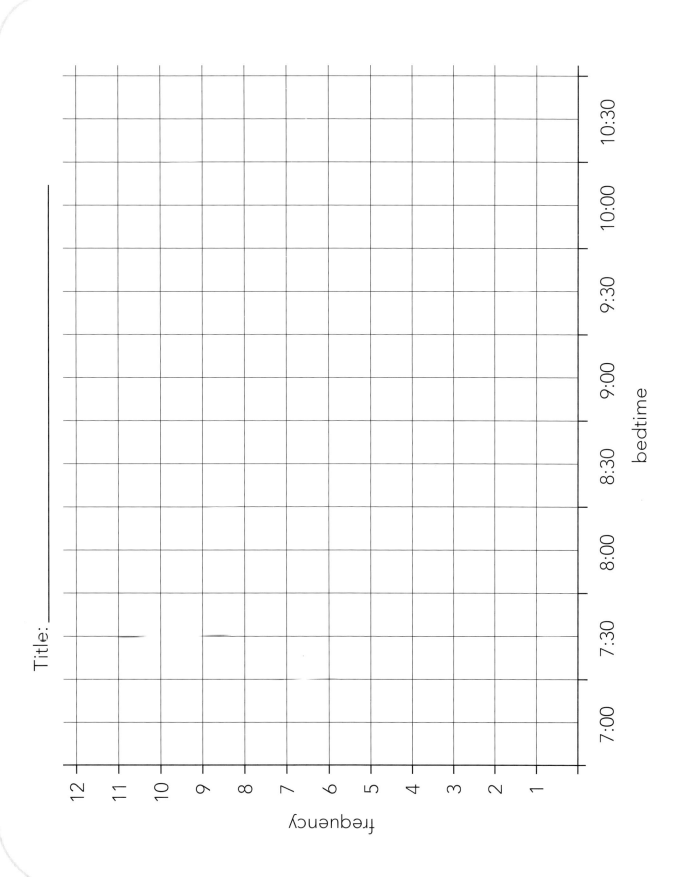

Title: _____

frequency

12
11
10
9
8
7
6
5
4
3
2
1

7:00   7:30   8:00   8:30   9:00   9:30   10:00   10:30

bedtime

Bags of cubes

Names:

One bag has
___ red cubes and ___ green cubes.
The other bag has
___ red cubes and ___ green cubes.
But which is which?

Bag A

Draw	Colour	
	Red	Green
1		
2		
3		
4		
5		
6		
7		
8		
9		
10		
11		
12		
13		
14		
15		
16		
17		
18		
19		
20		

Bag B

Draw	Colour	
	Red	Green
1		
2		
3		
4		
5		
6		
7		
8		
9		
10		
11		
12		
13		
14		
15		
16		
17		
18		
19		
20		

Predicting

	After 5 draws	After 10 draws	After 15 draws	After 20 draws
Bag A	__ red __ green	__ red __ green	__ red __ green	__ red __ green
Bag B	__ red __ green	__ red __ green	__ red __ green	__ red __ green